ARCHITECTURAL
FOLIAGE

ARCHITECTURAL
FOLIAGE

Shape, Form and Texture of
Foliage Plants in Garden Design

JILL BILLINGTON

WARD LOCK

DEDICATION

In memory of Graham Bunting

AUTHOR'S ACKNOWLEDGEMENTS

I was most grateful for the opportunity to photograph some beautiful gardens, details of which have featured in this book. In particular I valued the personal kindness of Mrs Jill Cowley, Mrs Gunilla Pickard, Mr Tim Newbury and Mr Peter Rouse and the generosity of Mr Hugh Johnson and Mrs Hannah Peschar for allowing me access to their gardens.

I also greatly appreciated the assistance with the preparation of the book from my husband and from Mrs Jayne Ball.

First published in Great Britain in 1991
by Ward Lock Limited, Villiers House,
41/47 Strand, London WC2N 5JE, England
A Cassell Imprint
© Ward Lock Ltd

Text filmset in Bembo 10/12pt
by Columns Design and Production Services Ltd, Reading
Printed and bound in Spain
by Graficromo

British Library Cataloguing in Publication Data
Billington, Jill
Architectural foliage.
1. Gardens : Landscape design
I. Title
712.6

ISBN 0 7063 6962 9

(Page 1) Delicately pointed fresh green shapes of the uncurling fronds of Matteuccia struthiopteris in spring, rising dramatically from the young foliage bed of Epimedium versicolor. The peeling cinnamon coloured bark of a young Acer griseum can be seen to the right.

(Page 3) A gently coloured border in which the tall red berberis, echoed by the mound of purple sage beautifully shows off a lime green euphorbia. The spots of crimson roses add great distinction.

CONTENTS

INTRODUCTION

ONCE the hunters and gatherers of our prehistoric past settled down and stayed put, sowing seed and reaping the benefit became an essential focus of life. From this developed twin pleasures of hands on the earth and enhancing surroundings. How to grow became a science and how to beautify progressed alongside. Every gardener loves his plants and learns how to care for them. He also loves his garden creatively and derives deep pleasure from making his own 'little bit of heaven'. This book is basically concerned with the latter.

Given our own space to play with, an open-air retreat which can be made beautiful is one of the great pleasures of life. Our plot may be small or large, rectangular or random; there may be practical limitations to be understood or overcome; but the creative drive to achieve our personal paradise will not let up until we are satisfied, if that is a possible outcome.

We gradually determine our aim by moulding this space, making it alive with shapes and patterns, enriched with texture and colour. However, thinking things through can save an awful lot of time, expense and disappointment. It is worth tackling first the 'skeleton' of the garden in visual terms. I have put on one side the delicious seduction of flowers and concentrated upon the form, decoration and texture of foliage plants. The elements of these are the shapes of leaves, both individually and in the mass.

In cities, which have had space and time for planning, architectural form becomes visible and enhanced, but the hotch potch of many old cities shows how distressingly easy it is to lose sight of fine architectural individuals. So too in the garden. Therefore, how to group, to display and to enhance is discussed. Practicality requires a realistic assessment of what you have and also what you would like. There are so many beauties to choose that considered selection is necessary to curb over-indulgence, but this creates the problem of such exhaustive choices that the examples are limited. The inclusion of plants which are not fully hardy is also a rather vexed issue. I have, therefore, indicated where necessary if plants are vulnerable to freezing temperatures. A great many 'indoor' plants have distinctive architectural form, but only a few of these, which can be moved out of doors in summer, have been mentioned.

To assist with such selection of plant material, the earlier sections of the book sift through the potential of shapes and forms. Leaves are described in artistic terms and whole plants are seen as three-dimensional sculpture. This should be of help when composing the garden plan. Diagrams are included to show plant forms and combinations in a schematic manner and shapes are pared down simplistically. This enables us to see and classify plants for practical and aesthetic arrangement. Are low horizontals needed in one part of the garden?

Fig. 1. The diagram emphasises the great diversity of forms available amongst garden plants.

Perhaps mounding rounded shapes are required. Is there a lack of focus; a need for a place for the eye to rest, an area to be hidden? Perhaps a dramatic accentuating vertical shape should be placed three quarters of the way up the garden then emphasized by repeating it elsewhere. Alternatively, the garden may be crying out for some massed planting to divert attention from the rectangularity of the plot. It may be that the garden is pretty but bland in which case some spiky eccentrics may enliven the scene. These are the sorts of questions which we first need to formulate by looking at what we have and then, using the diagrams and information in the book, resolve. Figure 1 gives some idea of the sort of shapes and patterns possible for a rectangular garden, making a balanced interesting unity.

Sometimes the detailed intricacy and beauty, observed and admired at close quarters, makes it difficult to see the plant as a whole. It is necessary to stand back to realize the impact such plants make when viewed from a distance. This is a crucial element of the designed garden scheme. By simplifying plant shapes to almost abstract form, as shown diagrammatically on p. 7 the plant masses become much easier to cope with. Planning the juxtaposition of trees, shrubs and perennials is less confusing. Of course other considerations, like the suitability of colour, aspect and soil type, have to be taken into account, but initially, judging the plant material as simple sculptural forms helps enormously with selection.

All art is about selection, but choice is a sophisticated concept. It is only natural to look in a sweet shop window and want it all. So resist making your selection in a Garden Centre. To achieve satisfying results it is necessary to make decisions; what to choose, and harder still, what to leave out. You cannot wear all your jewellery at once and expect to be pleased with the result.

Nevertheless, we are sometimes attracted to stylishly 'different' plants and cannot resist owning them. Plants like the dramatic yuccas, oriental bamboos and exotic palms, have great charisma, or perhaps we want highly individual plants of character, like the huge silvered Scotch thistle or lushly fronded tree fern.

A chapter has been specifically given over to such individuals, that is, plants with particularly stylish architectural form, described here as 'prima donnas'. These important characters can add enormously to the excitement and, dare I say, prestige, of the garden plan. Here again though, selection is the key. Horticultural specifics will rule out some anyway, but we must too, curb the temptation to over-indulge. The use of prima donnas as focal points means that consideration must also be given as to how they are best displayed. To do them justice, the accompanying plants should be chosen to flatter and foil rather than compete. This is discussed further in the relevant chapter.

In later chapters the relationship of foliage material to specific garden style or horticultural dictates are discussed: which plants look well in the romantic garden; how formality can be emphasized with the right choices; how certain plants set a scene, such as exotic or perhaps oriental. Suitability for people's domestic requirements is also referred to. It is useful to recognize that some plants lend themselves particularly well to man-made structures. We have also to consider which plants conceal the worst and reveal the best. How can courtyards be enhanced, boundaries adorned, and domestic architecture be flattered? These factors include situations which face many of us.

Within the book, I also outline the problems which occur when plants have to accommodate to restrictive situations, that is, when the going gets tough and there is an excess of sun and dry soil, or alternatively, a dank darkness to be lightened. These problems are addressed, but, for greater detail, other books will need to be consulted. There are many excellent books on horticultural practice so I do not want to complicate the issue here, by including too much of this information. If plants will not survive unless, for example, the soil is acidic or very damp, these factors have been mentioned, but the essence of the book

A finely mounding specimen Acer palmatum *'Dissectum Atropurpureum'. The spring sunlight draws attention to the elegance of its form.*

is to concentrate on the idea of foliage plants as the modelling clay or paints of an aesthetic endeavour and all that this implies.

The architectural theme inevitably drew me to trees and conifers as well as shrubs and herbaceous perennials and I have thus included a few of both.

Therefore my selection for the book has been necessarily restricted. Added to this, I admit to prejudices, but have tried not to let myself be too influenced by them. I know that my prejudices alter each year, as with all of us, but gardens are so personal that it is inevitable that likes and dislikes should crop up.

The passion for growing does not seem to let up from generation to generation. Now, with the twentieth century's inheritance from the great plant hunters and hybridists, horticultural offerings are richly, bewilderingly varied. Choices have to be made, and considering foliage for its architectural attributes enables the gardener to create a satisfying framework and dynamic impact within the garden.

Unlike architecture, a garden is always evolving. Plants outgrow their allotted spaces. Adaptation and change in relation to the basic framework provides a continuing challenge.

1
THE SHAPE OF
THE LARGER LEAF

A well planned garden is one where the line and mass are confidently balanced. Some plants have a naturally sculptural form, often markedly symmetrical. Others can be amorphous with no distinct shape at all. Verticals and horizontals always catch the eye and dominate a view. The softer rounded forms are a contrast providing a quieter image, but this is, literally, taking the long view.

Gardens are also places of decorative detail, particularly in the smaller gardens of today, where not only is the solid form of the plant significant but equally noticeable is the rich diversity of shapes and textures of the larger leaves. As this book is concerned with the visual aspect of gardening, the leaf shapes are classified simply on aesthetic rather than horticultural terms so that the architectural propensities are easily identified.

SPIKES

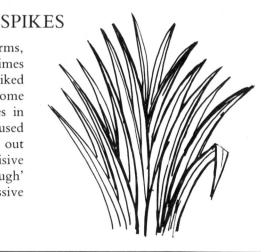

One of the most powerful forms, always eye-catching and sometimes exotic, is the erect, sword-like, spiked leaf. Foliage like this can provide some of the most dramatic punch lines in the business, but it can also be used merely to arrest the eye, to sort out over-rich patterns or to add a decisive formality, to say 'enough is enough' amongst the clamour of excessive foliage diversity.

Grouped foliage patterns at a Chelsea Flower Show garden designed by Tim Newbury. This shows foliage in a rich variety of shapes, textures and colours, beautifully grouped. Note the juxtaposition of round and narrow leaves and the effective duplication of shapes using different plants.

Rich textural tapestry effects of foliage alongside a brook lead the eye towards a specimen phormium backed by grasses.

The spears of the yuccas are sharply dangerous to look at. They pierce their way upward. This is no place for young children. *Yucca filamentosa* is as dramatically spiked as a plant can be. *Eryngium decaisneana* is another rapier-like dramatic plant which should be handled only with protective gloves, very striking but so painful.

Just as visually effective but distinctly kinder are the varieties of *Phormium tenax*. This magnificent, tall New Zealand shrub is now widely available. It has smooth grey-green leaves, creating a clarity of dramatic outline. The spikes can reach to 3 m (9 ft). With this architectural simplicity they dominate their peers, creating a focus in a town garden or drawing the eye in a mixed border. However, phormiums are not fully hardy and must have protection in very cold winters. *Phormium cookianum* is smaller and has softer leaves. The rigid sword shape is less pronounced as the leaves are lax and of a gentler habit. Though less spectacular, it is nevertheless an eye-catching sight and there are many strikingly stylish varieties of colour and size worth finding.

Formally displayed, Cordyline australis *'Albertii' looks magnificent under the dark wood pergola and framed by gentle acers.*

Another shrub which positively bristles with spiky foliage is *Cordyline australis*. Sometimes grown as a branching tree in milder districts, it can also be container grown and brought in for winter. Isolated in its container home, the lush, arching grass-like foliage is seen at its best, sculpturally dominant and richly, glossily green.

Despite being a native of South Africa, *Crocosmia masonorum* is a hardy herbaceous plant. The leaves provide tall swords of a fresh green. They are long, ribbed and slim, reaching a height of over a metre, incisively effective amongst other massed foliage. Careful siting is important to allow for the extremely vivid orange-red flowers in summer. Closely allied to the Crocosmia, and also from South Africa, *Curtonus paniculatus* 'Major' is magnificently sword-like. It too carries vivid orange-red sprays of flowers.

Spiky by profile but the contrary by nature, the gentle iris belongs in this group. Growing anywhere and everywhere, there is an iris for every situation both horticulturally and aesthetically. *Iris germanica* varieties, cultivated so easily and seen in every garden, have the most beautiful cool grey-green foliage. Massed together, fronting a bed of leggy shrub roses or edging a path, erect, confident fans of strap-shaped pointed leaves provide a positively lush but restful simplicity. The flowers, the origin of the 'fleur de lys', are the icing on the cake, despite a short flowering period.

Some irises must have moisture and even be grown in a few inches of water. Amongst these, *Iris kaempferi* has quantities of slender ribbed leaves 1 m (3 ft) tall. *Iris laevigata* is smaller and has smooth pale green slim leaves. The latter also has a very pretty and elegant variegated form. Both originate in the Far East. *Iris pseudacorus*, however, is a native of Europe. If planted in water up to a depth of 45 cm (1½ ft), its graceful grey-green leaves can reach an elegant 1.5 m (5 ft). The variegated form is stunningly beautiful.

Another delightful iris, *Iris pallida*, creates a sun-ray of soft greyish pointed leaves. There are exquisite cream or white variegated varieties. Ideal for formal planting or front of border, they are grown for the beauty of foliage as the flower is relatively undistinguished.

Before I leave the irises I must refer to an underused but invaluable species, *Iris foetidissima*. This European plant has shiny green strap-like leaves throughout the year. It will grow in full shade or sun and in any soil. The simple flowers are cream or blue but the pods of orange-red seeds make this iris an asset in autumn and winter. The variegated form is also evergreen and thus doubles its value in dark corners or in dry areas under trees, supplying lush, grass-like foliage, striped creamy-green, in dense but lax clumps.

Many irises grow in a fan-shaped two-dimensional pattern but a distant cousin, *Sisyrinchium striatum*, has a more three-dimensional growth habit. The attractive grey-green linear pointed leaves are roughly 45 cm (1½ ft) tall and grow erectly from the centre. Creamy flowers appear in early summer clustered around the length of the stem rods and emphasizing the vertical habit. The foliage is also evergreen but must be grown in sun. The variegated form, though slightly shorter, is especially charming, particularly in a paved garden.

REEDS

Not all plants with pointed narrow leaves are erect and spiky. Many create far softer, sometimes lax forms. The leaves are not starchily stiff but gently arched, flowing and curving, sometimes to the ground. The effect is quite different. Even the huge *Miscanthus sacchariflorus* which reaches for the sky, growing 3 m (9 ft) in one season, is softened by the waterfall of rustling leaves. *Arundo donax*, another powerfully tall, reedy plant also tempers its strong verticality with

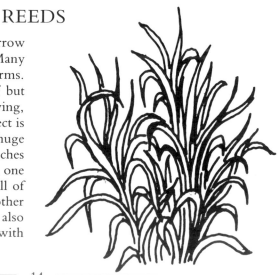

The glossy foliage of Phyllostachys bambusoides, *a bamboo noted for its large wide leaves.*

long wide grey floating foliage on alternate sides. Though the foliage of bamboos is carried on stiff erect canes, the leaves themselves create falls of gracefully soft curves. Many of the taller bamboos are used for screening, but others make superb ornamental individuals when displayed alone. One of the noblest, *Phyllostachys bambusoides*, carries leaves which can be 19 cm (8 in) long by 3 cm (1.5 in) wide. In cooler climes this bamboo reaches to over 4 m (13 ft) but a slightly smaller bamboo *Phyllostachys nigra* 'Boryana' is equally ornamental having purple-black canes, although its leaves are much finer. Known for having smaller leaves, *Arundinaria murielae* is a most graceful tall bamboo. The arching clumps have masses of slim leaves which can look quite feathery from a distance. Extremely elegant and growing to over 3.5 m (11½ ft), *Arundinaria nitida* is a star performer in isolation. The canes are flushed purple and the leaves are slim and delicate, again creating a soft hazy look from a distance.

Some dwarf bamboos tend to have wider leaves. *Sasa veitchii* is a rampant traveller and grows to a maximum of 1.2 m (4 ft). It has leaves as wide as 6 cm (2½ in) and up to 2.5 cm (10 in) long. The edges wither to a pale buff colour which from a distance creates a graphic pattern reinforcing the leaf outline. This can be attractive in winter, although on close inspection they can look rather tatty. *Sasa palmata* has the same type of wide-leaved foliage with die-back behaviour, but reaches 2.5 m (8 ft) and is even more rudely invasive. Slightly less inclined to mob rule, one of the prettiest garden bamboos is *Arundinaria viridistrata*. Fortunately very hardy, this plant grows to approximately 2 m (6 ft) or less and has long narrow golden-green foliage. It too tends to make too much lateral progress but is more easily restrained and is worth the effort. There is more detail about bamboos later.

Many of the grasses contrast superbly with their sword-like peers. They stir and flow in the wind. The huge pampas grasses such as *Cortaderia selloana*, with tousled slim reeds, can only be grown as specimens or together in groups. They are too dominating to blend. On the other hand the 120 cm (4 ft) high *Elymus arenarius* (lyme grass) is wickedly invasive, so, despite its graceful blue-grey linear curves, it too has to be sited with great care.

This is a tall but non-invasive bamboo, Arundinaria murielae. *The light green small, fluttery leaves are massed creating quite a different textural effect than that of* Phyllostachys bambusoides *seen in the previous photograph. Here they are showing off a wood sculpture by Reece Ingram.*

However, *Miscanthus sinensis* 'Gracillimus', growing to 150 cm (5 ft), has very fine, gracefully arching foliage. It can work well with the dense heavier forms of some shrubs, lightening a possible sombre effect.

Although heavier and less susceptible to wind, the decorative, reflexed narrow leaves of *Astelia nervosa* are a worthwhile addition. The leaves arch in a rosette discipline from the centre and are a satiny silver-grey. This New Zealand plant grows in 60 cm (2 ft) high tussocks which are 1.5 m (5 ft) wide and is evergreen.

Growing from 1 m (3 ft) to 1.2 m (4 ft) the day lilies, the Hemerocallis varieties, grow in clumps of light green, softly grassy foliage throughout the growing season, produce delicate lilies and are completely hardy. The more tender *Dierama pulcherrimum* must also be included. Known as the wand flower or Venus' fishing rods, its long, slim arching grassy leaves can reach 1.5 m (5 ft). Later in the summer, wands carrying drooping pink bell-flowers echo the form, making this a stunning plant to grow in paved isolation or over a pool. Wherever it is placed it must have a spacious flat surface around to reveal its natural grace.

ROUNDS

As a complete contrast to the swords and reeds described, there are large rounded leaves, sometimes so immense that they exclude all around them. When smaller, however, they can be calmly simple amongst over-rich, complicated foliage. Mostly deciduous, round leaves tend to grow fast during the season, creating overlapping discs serene in their simplicity.

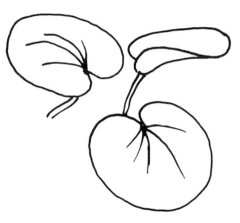

The largest rounded leaf form used in gardens is that of the massive, ragged edged *Gunnera manicata*. It must grow beside water, with no spatial restrictions. Slightly smaller, but equally greedy for space, is another water-loving plant *Petasites peltiphyllum*. The photograph of petasites on p. 44 shows these huge round leaves creating dramatic planting along a meandering brook. As with the even more massive gunnera, these are only for wet places in the largest gardens. *Peltiphyllum peltatum* (the umbrella plant of California) is more manageable. Each circular leaf is supported by its own stem and rises a metre from the marshy ground. Interestingly, this plant produces distinctive pink flower heads which also grow on stalks but appear early in the year, long before any foliage.

More realistically for the average garden is the round foliage of *Ligularia dentatum* 'Desdemona'. These too must not dry out. The strong, leathery foliage, uncompromisingly rounded, reveals deep maroon undersides when disturbed by wind. Some varieties are a very dark, almost metallic, green. They soothe the palate fed with an over-rich diet of mixed foliage. Yet again requiring moist soil, *Rodgersia tabularis* offers fully rounded foliage, as the stem is central to the leaf form. These very large leaves, however, are a soft light green and appear almost fragile if compared with the sturdy ligularia.

I shall take liberties with the word round to include worthies such as bergenia and brunnera. Both are so broad and rounded that their importance in garden design is that they provide simple patterns. *Bergenia cordifolia* varieties are amongst the most useful plants for any style of garden. Not only do they cope with shade and sun, drought and wind but they are also glossily evergreen. The boldly simple rounded forms at ground level grow where hostas would not thrive and accentuate the prettier foliage of astilbes or aquilegias and later in the year can be used to enclose more exuberant foliage patterns such as the Japanese anemones. Some bergenias have bright green shiny leaves but others can be purple, red and bronze, changing during the year.

The glossy rounded leaves of Asarum europaeum. *This small woodland plant will grow beneath trees and provides a light-reflecting attractive pattern of roundels suited to the intimacy of small town gardens. The leaves of* Helleborus orientalis, Hosta seiboldiana *and* Vinca minor *'Aureovariegata' are just visible.*

The wide heart-shaped leaves of *Brunnera macrophylla*, can be used for the same effect. The summer foliage, undemanding to the eye, provides a simple backcloth at ground level for more luxuriant plants and will cover areas of damp shade. The pretty blue forget-me-not flowers attract attention in spring before the leaves have reached their full size. There is an extremely attractive variety, 'Hadspen Cream', a variegated form, which is worth looking for.

Also suited to ground cover use is glossy leaved *Galax urceolata (Galax aphylla)* which, unlike brunnera, is evergreen. It grows well in woodland conditions where the 8 cm (3 in) diameter circular leaves overlap one another and acquire reddish colouring in winter. At a lower level, a mere 2 cm (½ in) high, *Asarum europaeum*, seen in the photograph on p. 18, also has neat rounded highly glossed evergreen leaves. Growing in cooler shady moist sites it provides a contrasting foil to more wayward foliage, such as the shade-loving ferns.

BROAD

As with rounded or sword-shaped leaves, the wide and pointed classic broad leaf shape, loosely encompassing ovate and elliptic form, is effectively simple. The broad leaf form is common in nature but has many permutations. The hardy evergeen aucubas, rhododendrons, skimmias, viburnums and laurels provide simple undistracting backcloths of neat elliptic foliage.

Stout-hearted *Aucuba japonica* grows anywhere and is thus used in much municipal planting, but look again. The foliage is green, speckled or variegated and even narrowly lanceolate. It is a trusty. *Prunus laurocerasus*, the laurel, is nearly as valuable, with many, widely differing, named varieties, some adapting to nearly impossible situations. Rhododendrons when not in flower provide a visually undemanding but evergreen darkness. They must have acid, free-draining but moist soil. Generally, the larger the leaf, the greater the shade required. Some have magnificent leaves, for example *Rhododendron sinogrande*, which is really a small tree and has leaves nearly a metre long. If you do not live in an area which would naturally support them, however, they can look false amongst other plants. Isolate the smaller ones in containers in ericaceous soil and they suit the town garden, but dump them amidst the ordinary mixed shrub and herbaceous bed and they never will look right. They should be seen mounding up the sides of a woodland valley, where they are well suited to their environment.

A shrub with ovate foliage which I have used in nearly every garden plan is *Viburnum davidii*. Of Chinese origin, this is a hardy, neat and evergreen shrub. The elliptic foliage is a dark glossy ribbed green. It will be mentioned again.

Bamboos may generally be thought of as grassy but *Sasa veitchii* carries very large broad elliptic leaves in layers of greedy ground cover. The leaves blanch around the margins emphasizing the shape and creating linear patterns when viewed from a distance. It must be severely contained or planted in large spaces.

Of course, not only shrubs have elliptic foliage. Many herbaceous plants offer the simple charm of this leaf form. A pride of hostas can make the most ordinary herbaceous bed distinctive. The sculptured foliage, encouraging to see in spring, has a no-nonsense dignity about it. Continuing through the year it grows in orderly layers, cooling down the competing textures, shapes and colours of the surrounding scene. *Hosta sieboldiana* 'Elegans' is one of the most magnificent, having the largest leaves which can be up to 30 cm (1 ft) wide. Over the years it establishes a confident layered mound of grey-blue richly ribbed leaves.

Hostas make superb contrasts against lacy foliage and can anchor more soaring verticals firmly to the ground. *Hosta undulata* creates a rippling effect. *Hosta fortunei* 'Albopicta' has a spectacularly colourful leaf. *Hosta lancifolia* is narrowly pointed. *Hosta* 'Francee' has a wide heart-shaped leaf reinforced with pure white edging. Two smaller hostas are completely different from one another: 'Ginko Craig' has small lance-shaped white-margined leaves and 'Halcyon' has pointed silvery grey ones. The possibilities are unlimited, it seems, and the hybridists are hard at work to satisfy the passionate hosta collector.

Sophisticated design is often simple and this is the outstanding virtue of the hosta family. The leaves can be deeply engraved with linear veining and may be either slimly pointed or broadly rounded. The complex permutations of variegated colour patterns, as well as plain greens, yellow and blue-greys add to their versatility. As foliage plants the Hosta family fits in with many styles. Invaluable in shaded ferny woodland, they will also suit the more architectural demands of patios. They can even look very well in containers provided the conditions are right. One note of caution: beware the slug and snail or your sculptural hostas will join the class of lacy foliage.

In areas where the heat would deny the hosta its lush growth, *Trachystemon orientale*, a member of the borage family, will provide similarly handsome large heart-shaped leaves. These overlap like the hosta but do not have the rosette-like pattern. They are coarsely hairy and very invasive but can be useful where other large leaves would fail.

In contrast, I have a great affection for the delicate epimediums and am using an artist's licence to group them amongst elliptic foliage. Their heart-shaped asymmetrical leaflets are suspended in tiers above one another by fine wiry stems. I am touched by their fragile appearance which belies the fact that they are completely hardy and some are evergreen. They establish themselves slowly in mounds and possess a delicacy and fineness of form and colour which contrasts greatly with the more plastic moulding of the hosta. *Epimedium perralderianum* is a useful evergreen but should be trimmed in late winter to allow the flowers to be raised to their suspended height, later followed by young hovering leaves. Preferring shade, they will grow in sun but more

Polygonatum giganteum *arches over the delicate heart-shaped leaves of epimedium.*

Dramatic pleated Veratrum *leaves are extremely handsome in the shaded border.* Asperula
odorata *is a pretty accompanying ground cover.*

A group of hostas showing variation of glaucous greens and contrasting with the glossy foliage of bergenia. Further away are two greatly differing ligularias, one having smoothly rounded leaves with red undersides named Ligularia dentatum 'Desdemona' *and the other,* Ligularia stenocephala *which has jaggedly toothed foliage.*

slowly. The foliage of some epimediums is enhanced by delicious garnishing of burgundy red. *Epimedium rubrum*, though deciduous, is extremely pretty when young, with yellow veins tracing across the deep red leaves. These fragile leaves belong in any garden but are particularly well suited to clothing the foot of trees in a layer of moisture-retaining humus.

Contrast the lightness of epimediums with the dignified aristocratic veratrum. These regal plants grow vertically at least to 1.2 m (4 ft) and, in the case of the North American *Veratrum viride*, reach 2 m (7 ft). They must have moist conditions and shade but have magnificently ribbed ovate leaves growing from the base of the plant which should not be covered. *Veratrum nigrum* is especially striking. The leaves unfold from a fan of pleats and the narrow spikes of flowers are a dramatic black-purple.

NARROW

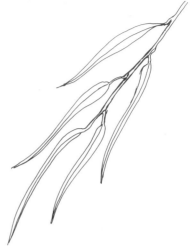

A narrow type of classic foliage is called lanceolate. This elegant foliage deserves a separate grouping. The line is voguishly slim. The evergreen *Prunus laurocerasus* 'Zabeliana' is a wide, horizontally branched, low evergreen with tapering slim leaves. It provides striking ground cover in shade or sun.

Some cotoneasters also have willow-like narrow pointed foliage. The pattern on paving created by the wandering prostrate *Cotoneaster salicifolius* 'Repens' creates a satisfyingly graphic design particularly when aided by some subtle pruning. The 4 m parent, *Cotoneaster salicifolius*, traces similar elegant patterns against the sky.

Another reliable go-anywhere evergreen shrub, *Aucuba japonica* 'Salicifolia', has remarkably slim dark foliage enhanced in winter by clustering, red berries.

A very beautiful herbaceous plant, which is not grown often enough is *Gentiana asclepiadea*, the willow gentian. This European plant has a most stylish growth pattern. It arches to nearly a metre in height and there are pairs of lanceolate leaves along the slim wand. In late summer these are emphasized by pairs of rich blue gentian flowers. A moist, partially shaded site is essential. It is well shown gracefully arching down over the wall of a raised bed. It gathers momentum over the years if left undisturbed.

Of course, willows are a major part of this group. *Salix alba* 'Sericea', actually a small tree, can be grown as a small shrub if pruned early in the year to about 1 m (3 ft) in height. *Salix exigua* is equally lovely. Both have slender silver-silk foliage which catches the breeze with trembling vivacity. Beware that the latter is rampant.

Named after the willow, *Pyrus salicifolia* 'Pendula' is a loved small garden tree. Actually a small pear tree, it is grown for its delightful weeping habit with linear silvery leaves creating an insubstantial floating foliage. It is highly suitable for small gardens, bringing light and grace to a paved garden or attracting romantics when planted with shrub roses, irises and lavenders.

Quite different in character but carrying even slimmer grey foliage, *Hippophae rhamnoides* is a large shrub, native to the British Isles. The presence of spines make it distinctly more hawkish than dovelike. The slim grey leaves make a light textural contribution rather than create a mood. This practical shrub grows well as a maritime windbreak and has the attraction of masses of orange berries, provided there are enough males to females.

The pines should be mentioned here. The small *Pinus mugo* and lush *Pinus strobus* 'Nana' suit paved gardens where their needle-like growth creates a touch of oriental charm.

FEATHERY

Some foliage is so finely formed that the total effect is feathery, even hazy. Individual leaves do not signify. The insubstantial softness of the leaves adds a romantic feeling to a garden. *Tamarix pentandra* creates a grey haze of foliage clouding around the branches. This small tree is also well suited to coastal districts but I find it difficult to place in a garden in a satisfactory way. I suspect that I don't actually like it. Fennel, *Foeniculum vulgare*, growing as a haze of green or brown-red is a culinary herb, increasingly used for its design potential. Again, I am not susceptible to its charms.

However, the artemisias I love. This wonderful genus of feathery-leaved grey, silver and green foliage types has much to offer. *Artemisia* 'Powys Castle' has a silvery filigree foliage nearly 1 m (3 ft) tall and hardy. This is a plant which adds lightness of touch to stately regal lilies, shooting delphiniums, powerful acanthus and so on. It can be used as an echoing emphasis for the billow of gypsophila or frothy curds of *Hydrangea paniculata* 'Grandiflora'. Half the size, *Artemisia canescens* is a silvery mass of lace.

Some of the artemisias are less feathery in leaf. *Artemisia ludoviciana* 'Latifolia' is a tall 60 cm (2 ft) form with broader leaves. It is known as 'white sage' in its North American home. The finest filigree leaf of all the artemisias is *Artemisia arborescens*, 'Faith Raven' being the hardiest form. As this plant comes from southern Europe it prefers hot sun and very free-draining soil. Just one night of frozen wet soil around the base and it is done for. Pruning to the ground in early spring is recommended to produce massed tiny filaments of silvery foliage. Otherwise you may find that you have a rather miserable top-heavy leggy plant. Most of the artemisias require this care and some must be protected in winter. I cannot resist mentioning a great favourite, although it is very small, only 8 cm (3 in) high: *Artemisia schmidtiana* 'Nana' is a compact mound of silvery feathery moss. It looks beautiful in raised planting, shimmering silver as it spills over a wall.

Some of the beautiful maples have feathery foliage. *Acer palmatum* 'Dissectum' varieties are softly domed shapes which weep elegantly creating a flutter of feathery leaves. They look graceful associated with still or moving water, in front of dense dark rhododendrons or trailing softly down the wall of a raised bed in a town garden.

Somewhat similar to the dissectum group of acers, there are some familiar shrubs which have choice lacy foliage varieties. *Sambucus nigra* 'Laciniata' (fern-leaved elder) is a pretty shrub, tall and wide, with finely incised leaves which stir in the slightest whisper of wind. The over-used sumach has a very pretty form *Rhus glabra* 'Laciniata' which also has flowing foliage floating above other more prosaic shrubs.

The soft fronds of ferns are included in later sections of the book, but I must refer to them here for their useful adaptability. Artemisias need sun but many ferns will grow in the darkest of corners. They can add an air of feathery frivolity to the serious shrubs of the shade garden. They contrast well with the other shade-suited herbaceous plants which are the more sculpturally defined forms of the hellebores, brunnera, bergenia and hostas.

TWINNED

A major decorative group of leaf forms includes the pinnate shapes, most familiar in the ash tree. Twinned leaves repeat along the stem simply, as shown, or duplicated again, in which case they are known as bipinnate.

Amongst the shrubs, *Sorbaria aitchisonii* is very tall and elegant, growing in large thickets and looking well when associated with water. In summer it has the prettiest light frothy panicles of creamy flowers. Hard pruning in late winter produces extra large foliage.

Even taller and with larger pinnate foliage is the distinctive Japanese angelica tree, *Aralia elata*. This creates quite a different pattern as its leaves tend to grow in a ruff around the ends of the branches. The suckering habit produces a small forest of stems with a canopy of huge bipinnate leaves through which sunlight flickers upon the plants below. The variegated version is extremely beautiful. Both are enhanced with fluffy foaming panicles of white flowers in early autumn.

The great tree of heaven, *Ailanthus altissima* can be grown as a shrub by coppicing. It will produce a shrub 2–3 m (6–10 ft) high in a season with very long dramatic pinnate foliage. It appears far more dense and heavy than either the sorbaria or the aralia.

Many trees, including the robinias, some sorbus, *Sophora japonica* and others, display elegantly pinnate foliage which can be a more delicate choice for a garden than some of the more heavy blossom trees which are not noteworthy except in spring.

I must mention also the wistarias whose charming pinnate leaves justify growing of these climbers, even though they are usually grown for their exquisite trailing flowers. Monet's bridge at Giverny is beautifully clad from spring to autumn with wistaria, whereas the flowering period is one month only.

At ground level, the divided pinnate fronds of the ferns create structured patterning. Great favourites in Victorian times, their popularity has increased again now that 'easy-care' foliage plays such a major part in contemporary gardens. Under trees or in shady areas, they require space to reveal their graceful symmetry. The choice must be affected by the conditions. *Osmunda regalis*, the royal fern, attains a magnificent 120 cm (4 ft) when grown in peaty, boggy land. It contrasts superbly with the huge sword-shaped flag iris or the rounded petasites. The proud lacy fronds of *Matteuccia struthiopteris*, the ostrich feather fern, must also grow in wet soil. They look well with the damp-loving rodgersia varieties. Contrasting dramatically with smooth hostas, rosettes of *Euphorbia robbiae*, or the bold foliage of the hellebores, the shade-loving ferns enrich the textures of shade planting. The evergreen shield ferns, *Polystichum aculeatum* varieties, are very attractive. The common *Dryopteris filix-mas* will grow where no plant has grown before. It copes with hostile situations, such as under hedges and around the base of large trees. Combine the softness of the patterned pinnate ferns with rigidly solid mahonias and hollies for an easily maintained attractive effect.

As shown, pinnate foliage can be simply smooth or fussily feathery. It can also be dramatically prickly. A group of mahonias provides notable evergreen foliage. The prickly leaves of *Mahonia japonica* radiate out from the branches. Blessings of scented yellow racemes of flowers in winter followed by clusters of blue-bloomed berries add to the worth of these wonderful plants. *Mahonia lomariifolia* is admirable for its stately elegance but must have a sheltered site and protection. I am also partial to *Mahonia* 'Winter Sun' which is hardier, with its erect fragrant flowers and the less hardy *Mahonia* 'Lionel Fortescue', both of which are smaller than the magnificent *Mahonia lomariifolia*. These shrubs will add visual excitement to staid unsunny corners.

PALMATE

Amongst the most memorable foliage in any garden are the palmate type, commonly recognized in the horse chestnut. Some of these make such eye-catching dominating specimens that they do not relate comfortably to other plants. *Fatsia japonica, Crambe cordifolia, Ficus carica* and *Rheum palmatum* all need placing with care. They will be dwelt upon in greater detail in Chapter 2.

The well known digitate palmate leaf of the horse chestnut family can be found in shrub form. *Aesculus indica mutabilis* (Indian horse chestnut) and *Aesculus pavia* 'Atrosanguinea' (red

Always elegant in growth the acers offer a variety of beautiful leaf shapes.

buckeye) of North America make very large shrubs or small trees but *Aesculus parviflora* is smaller. All are suitable only for the larger garden where their beautiful leaves add distinction.

One of the greatest plant families for the artist gardener is the maple. Their natural grace and elegance make them irresistible. Do not be put off by some failures. Despite horticultural rules, acers call the tune and can be unpredictable. I have seen a red *Acer palmatum* glowing healthily, without a burnt leaf in sight, exposed to full sun and wind. Like children, acers do not read the books on how to bring them up and can innocently flourish where they should not. *Acer japonicum* varieties slowly grow to make small trees or delicate tall shrubs with pretty palmate foliage. *Acer japonicum* 'Vitifolium' has leaves which are fan-shaped, often with 10 lobes, creating a very delicate pattern and colouring richly in autumn. The palmatum species, casually referred to as the Japanese maple, also grows very slowly to small tree status. The finely palmate leaves, with five to seven lobes, are often deliciously coloured. Their decorative value lies in the paradox of lush foliage, which is nevertheless so light that the leaves lift in the slightest breeze revealing the elegance of the tree structure.

As this is not a book about maples I must restrict myself as to choice. The dissectum variation of *Acer palmatum* has already been mentioned but amongst the many other varieties there are some very beautiful plants. *Acer palmatum* 'Senkaki' (coral bark maple) is a lovely plant to own, particularly when the leaves colour in autumn. *Acer palmatum* 'Heptalobum Elegans' has sculpted leaves which burn a fiery red in the fall. Maples look their best when their fragile elegance is seen against heavier-leaved shrubs, particularly those which flower early and become depressing in later months. They can be exquisite as specimens in hard-paved gardens or flow beautifully over rocks and associate gently with water.

Amongst herbaceous plants which provide beautifully palmate foliage the rodgersias are the most striking. *Rodgersia tabularis* has already been noted for its round leaves but the leaves of *Rodgersia pinnata* radiate from the stem, thus appearing to be digitate. Those of *Rodgersia podophylla* and *Rodgersia aesculifolia*, also radiating from the stem, are deeply incised and palmate in style. They can be richly bronzed as the photograph on p. 85 shows, sometimes creating an almost metallic patina. Because the leaves are so large and carried on single thick stems nearly one metre high, these are markedly eye-catching foliage plants. They spread easily by rhizomes in rich damp soil and must be spaciously planted. Nevertheless, they are not too out of scale to be considered for the smaller garden where the impact of large leaves can be considerable. I like to place them with the late flowering *Cimicifuga racemosa* or the proudly magnificent *Aruncus sylvester*, but astilbes and hostas associate well. The fronds of the tall ferns and reedy leaves of the flag iris will also accommodate to the eye-catching rodgersias.

Hellebores belong to another sculpturally leaved herbaceous plant family which has palmate lobed glossy foliage. They will grow under trees or in north-facing borders, are winter-flowering and handsomely evergreen. I consider them to be indispensable in every garden style. *Helleborus corsicus* has the richest foliage, divided into threes but closely resembling palmate patterns. *Iris foetidissima*, plain and variegated, contrasts well as do the round brunnera leaves. A carpeting of *Anemone blanda* and primroses further the charm in spring and arching polygonatum and frondy ferns combine well as the season progresses.

Also trifoliate rather than palmate is the Mexican orange, *Choisya ternata*, which has surprisingly bright green foliage for an evergreen. For this reason alone it is invaluable, bringing fresh green to the garden in winter. The foliage is also very glossy, reflecting light into the dullest areas. The bonus of highly scented white blossom, sometimes twice a year, makes this a shrub to be prized. There are two new hybrid choisyas on the market, a yellow-leaved form called 'Sundance' and an extremely pretty narrow-leaved one named 'Aztec Pearl'. Usefully, choisyas will grow in sun or shade to a neat height of about 2 m (6 ft). However, they do need some protection in harsh climates.

There are some characterful climbers which have palmate-like foliage. The vine is always decorative and has a claret coloured form *Vitis vinifera* 'Purpurea', which graduates to a deep purple as autumn arrives. If you have the climate for grapes as well, you are blessed. The fruiting *Vitis* 'Brandt' is also tolerant of more modest climates. The three- to five-lobed leaves are green in summer but in autumn they become a rich maroon colour and their structure is very prettily delineated by yellow veining. *Parthenocissus henryana* has digitate leaves with three to five leaflets. Finely drawn veins decorate the matt dark green surface. By the autumn, the leaves have turned to a rich red. Note also *Parthenocissus quinquefolia*, the true Virginia creeper, which richly textures walls with brilliant scarlet at the end of the year. Be warned that this is a rampageous climber.

There are oddities of shape in the leaf world. Indeed my classifications have been greatly simplified and not botanically exact, but I am looking for patterns. I would therefore like to mention *Ginkgo biloba* (maidenhair tree), which is often referred to as a living fossil as its relatives can be found in Jurassic beds. It bears no resemblance to its peers, conifers, as it has deciduous fan-shaped leaves with primitive veining. As it is a narrow tree and is tolerant of pollution, some cities use it to line their streets; an interesting image beside modern technology.

The tulip tree, *Liriodendron tulipifera* has pale green leaves which are very wide, almost square, with two additional pointed lobes on either side. It is best seen as a specimen, but beware that it takes many years to flower.

Finally, I must mention *Salix matsudana* 'Tortuosa', a curiosity where the branches and leaves writhe into a twisted form. Pretty when adorned with snow in winter and fast growing, it has its uses. However, the similarly twisted *Corylus avellana* 'Contorta', the corkscrew hazel, is only attractive in winter when the catkins trail vertically from the twisted forms. I have to say that in summer the leaves merely look as if they have succumbed to a disease.

When planning a whole garden, a backyard or just an island bed, the diverse shapes and patterns of the larger leaf forms help to establish structure and balance. Looking to create unity, the gardener can find that contrasting and blending patterns of leaves will create vitality and harmony.

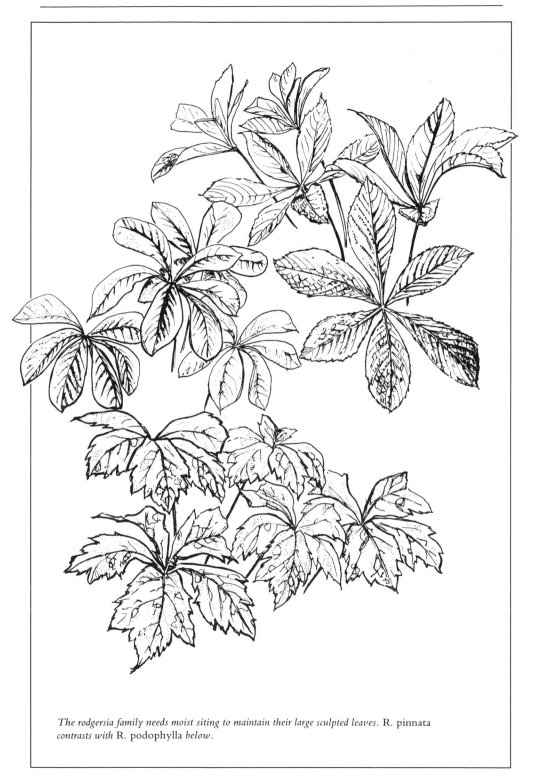

The rodgersia family needs moist siting to maintain their large sculpted leaves. R. pinnata
contrasts with R. podophylla *below.*

2
THE FORMS
CREATED BY
MASSED
FOLIAGE

SMALLER leaves, individually unremarkable, can create distinctive sculptural
forms, clarifying the design of a garden. An amorphous mass of mixed
foliage, however individually beautiful, can be boringly uninteresting if
there is no punch to catch the eye. Placing some verticals for impact, or
horizontals to lead the eye across a space, relieves the monotony of thoughtless
planting.

Although some shrubs have shape imposed upon them as topiary, most have
their own natural and distinctive form. This is dictated by the stem structure or
the density of leaf mass. It is useful to think of these as very simple shapes. The
diagrams on pp. 34–35 illustrate the essential silhouette.

VERTICALS

Amongst the natural forms the vertical
is the most eye catching. Narrowly
upright, or fastigiate, trees can be
extremely useful for those people who
garden in small spaces.

Prunus 'Amanogawa' and *Malus*
'Van Eseltine' are in demand as small
fastigiate trees. In a larger garden a
family group of three or five could be
most attractive. A large beech, *Fagus
sylvatica* 'Dawyck', creates a powerful
slender upright shape, but this is a
very tall tree suited only to spacious
places.

Given space, the magnificently huge incense cedar, *Calocedrus decurrens*, could be considerately planted for future generations whilst the smaller, faster *Chamaecyparis columnaris* 'Glauca' will satisfy the impatience of others. Many other conifers stand to attention but *Juniperus virginiana* 'Skyrocket', a very narrow grey pencil, *Juniperus communis* 'Hibernica' (Irish yew) and the dwarf *Juniperus communis* 'Compressa' are probably the most used. For my part, *Taxus baccata* 'Fastigiata' is indispensable. It is a very dark yew and adds a powerful columnar form which can be clipped if necessary. Whatever the seasonal disarray, the reassuring sentinels of yew add distinction. However, as I stated earlier, conifers and trees can only be peripheral in these pages, so I have resisted the temptation to dwell on them further.

On a smaller garden scale, *Rosmarinus officinalis* 'Fastigiatus', sometimes called 'Miss Jessop's Upright', provides a more informal vertical. It is a soft grey-green, lightened with pale blue flowers in early summer. Rosemary plants are slightly tender.

A most attractive ivy *Hedera helix* 'Erecta' is a tallish, free-standing evergreen. Very similar but marginally less robust and a little narrower, *Hedera helix* 'Congesta' is also a free-standing vertical small shrub. This one has more pointed and heavily veined leaves. Known as the 'candelabra' ivies for their rococo style they grow well in rockeries, raised beds or in town gardens where scale is extra important.

Both bamboos and grasses can provide highly satisfactory upright forms. Beware that the bamboos are not too invasive. A tall grass, *Miscanthus sacchariflorus* (also named *M. floridulus*) grows vertically to over three metres in one growing season. It must be cut down to the ground annually. The huge upright canes are softened by falls of grassy leaves which rustle continually in the slightest movement of air.

Amongst herbaceous plants there are many which grow into tall upright shapes, for example verbascum, eremurus, madonna lilies, foxgloves, kniphofia. If there are parallel verticals of a different scale elsewhere in the garden, these plants can create an interesting dialogue, changing throughout the growing season. Then again, the vertical theme could also be echoed in the pendulous catkins of *Garrya elliptica*, the swinging flower trails of *Itea ilicifolia* or the lengthy, beautiful racemes of wistaria.

HORIZONTALS

The horizontal line is observable at many levels. There are shrubs whose branches are virtually parallel to the ground creating layers of horizontal foliage. There is a most beautiful dogwood, *Cornus controversa* 'Varie-gata' and a lovely *Viburnum plicatum* 'Mariesii', both of which have a horizontally tiered form. The former,

Upright shapes are eye-catching. They provide focal points and are dramatic in the garden view. They are always dominant, even when part of a repeat pattern.

Horizontally layered plants can be used to create repeat patterns when massed. They have a tranquil effect and lead the eye elsewhere in the garden.

Many shrubs are rounded or dome-shaped. These provide the infilling structure for most gardens. Dense and compactly rounded forms are useful in the formal garden but also provide structural emphasis amongst more romantic, ill-disciplined foliage patterns.

Low, weeping mounded shapes act as a foil, anchoring vertical or dramatic foliage to the ground. These shapes are elegant and non-intrusive in the total pattern.

Fan-shaped forms provide a contrast to rounded or weeping shapes. The straight lines, fanning from a central pivot, hold sway above lower foliage patterns. When composed of reed-like pointed leaves the shape is extremely dramatic.

Very wide open fans are not eye-catching or dramatic but are receptive to other shapes. They lead the eye to other parts of the garden. Sometimes weeping tips create a softer, more romantic effect.

Large weeping forms attract attention and relate dramatically with the horizontal plane of water or lawn. They are romantic backgrounds, as well as being of interest in themselves.

Upright bowl-shapes look better when massed rather than as individuals. However, as part of a group, they contrast well with low weeping forms, horizontal and rounded ones.

Cornus controversa, which is of Chinese origin, is a remarkable beauty which develops into a small tree. The layered line is emphasized in early summer when it is flower laden along the wide branches. Similarly the viburnum splendidly emphasizes the horizontals with flat white lacy florets, also in early summer.

Prunus laurocerasus 'Zabeliana' is another shrub which grows parallel to the ground, but at a maximum height of 1 m (3 ft), cutting extremely wide evergreen swathes across space and it will grow just about anywhere. This plant has unusual candle-like white flowers in spring.

Very slightly taller, but of elegant and fairly horizontal habit, is an acid-loving shrub *Leucothoe fontanesiana*. It is not as stiff as the prunus and the curved branches carry pendant rather than erect racemes. This graceful evergreen grows happily in light shade with its ericaceous companions.

With smaller leaf texture but a low and wide branching habit *Lonicera pileata* is evergreen. Like *Cotoneaster horizontalis* it can be used as an underskirt for larger shrubs or to fan widely over paving.

At this low level, spreading conifers can duplicate this line. *Juniperus sabina* 'Tamariscifolia' is a most satisfying conifer as it grows tidily in flat concentric layers. Some of the prostrate conifers spread their wings over surprising distances when mature. Allowance should be made when planting. It is sad to see them hacked back, destroying their largess.

Associating well with conifers, a low growing broom, *Cytisus kewensis*, is a mass of radiating lines, bowed nearly horizontal by the weight of cream flowers in spring.

At true ground level the horizontal line becomes a carpet. Prostrate conifers can hug ground contours but so too can the creeping cotoneasters such as *Cotoneaster dammeri* or *Cotoneaster microphyllus cochleatus*. Never forget the many varieties of ivy which offer distinctive ground cover. The word mat is an accurate description, as the tiny ground-hugging thymes, sagina, cotula, chamomile, raoulia and similar alpines can actually be walked upon.

DOMES

Some plants are naturally round or dome shaped. The small leaves conform tidily within the shape providing round compact silhouettes. The hebes are particularly valuable for their neat sculputural contribution. They are from New Zealand but have become familiar in gardens throughout the world. *Hebe salicifolia* is one of the largest. Its bright green lanceolate leaves conform to a neat rounded mound, charmingly covered with lengthy racemes of white flowers in summer. Contrastingly, *Hebe albicans*

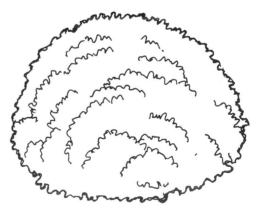

is a dwarf rounded form with glaucous foliage. One of the freshest evergreens in the garden is *Hebe rakiensis*. This valued hebe provides a grass-green bun-shaped form and is relatively hardy. On the other hand *Hebe salicifolia* 'Midsummer Beauty' must have protection. This particularly beautiful rounded shrub has leaves which are flushed with red and flowers of lavender purple.

The Japanese influenced clipped forms of Buxus sempervirens *resembling rounded boulders. This is a distinctive and unusual style of topiary.*

For tall rounded forms, trees like *Malus floribunda* (ornamental crabapples), *Robinia pseudoacacia* 'Inermis' (mop-headed acacia), and the hawthorn *Crataegus laciniata* are some which make rounded profiles at a higher level.

Many of the shrubby potentillas can provide quite neat domed forms which can be useful as they have the additional advantage of a long flowering season. *Potentilla fruticosa* 'Primrose Beauty' is a good example.

Although usually associated with hedging, *Ligustrum ovalifolium* 'Aureum' need not only be thought of as the dusty, if reliable, golden privet of town gardens. It is too good for this role only, as it is informally rounded and will grow virtually anywhere. It can also be clipped to a perfect round if required.

Some mid-height garden shrubs are quite rounded in form. *Choisya ternata* is a glossy evergreen, flowers twice a year and neatly reaches a height of 1.80 m (6 ft). Not quite so tidy but still dense and rounded *Viburnum tinus* is also evergreen and approximately 2–3 m (7–10 ft) tall.

Viburnum davidii is also an evergreen, rounded shrub about 1 m (3 ft) but it is oval rather than truly round, as the large leaves create a flatter pattern. Skimmias are more reliably neatly dome shaped, but need an acid soil.

Some of the conifers also qualify. *Chamaecyparis lawsoniana* 'Minima Glauca' is a small globe of rich green. Often the name 'globe' or 'dome' tells all amongst the small conifers.

A minimal rounded shrub, *Berberis thunbergii* 'Bagatelle', when planted en masse, creates attractive, red-leaved, rounded tussocks, no more than 30 cm (1 ft) high. These can provide an unusual ground-level surface for more daring, flamboyant overseers or alternatively, blend unobtrusively with azaleas, dwarf conifers, heathers and creeping grey-leaved alpine willows.

FANS

Quiet rounded forms can be a perfect foil for more dramatic fan-shaped shrubs. Many plants grow naturally from a crown and fan out to catch light and air. Some are exceptionally geometrical in form which can be of value to the designer. The sword-like phormiums and cordylines have already been described. Sisyrinchium and irises belong here too.

Some shrubs, like *Prunus laurocerasus* 'Otto Luyken', rise confidently from the ground ascending 45° from their base. Grouped together they create repeated fan patterns. Usefully, this plant will grow in inhospitable sites and is thus employed in a lot of municipal planting schemes.

Ferns also provide inverted cones as the fronds fan out from a central pivot. There is no better image of this than *Matteuccia struthiopteris* rising from boggy soil. Another magnificent fern from Asia, *Dryopteris wallichiana* is 150 cm (5 ft) high. It is truly an oriental beauty with perfect symmetry as the uncurling brilliant green fronds fan out from the crown. The humbler common fern from the British Isles, *Dryopteris filix-mas*, follows the same pattern. Growing anywhere, its versatility must be commended. Also from Britain, *Polystichum setiferum acutilobum* follows a spiral growth pattern around the crown and grows extremely elegantly, even in dry soil and through the winter.

The two-dimensional fans of the beautiful *Iris pallida* 'Variegata' must be mentioned again and the remarkably flat 'fan-upon-fan' growth pattern of *Cotoneaster horizontalis* should be included. The latter will reach up to a considerable height upon a wall and should be encouraged by trimming out any forward growing shoots. Alternatively, it can be grown as a link between wall and paving by allowing branches to fan downwards along the floor. It is a great pity that this shrub does not have an evergreen form.

BOWLS

Differing from the straight-sided fan is the curved bowl shape so characteristic of the dogwoods. *Cornus stolonifera* 'Flaviramea', if cut at ground level each spring, produces new shoots for the following winter, making a forest of greeny-yellow shoots. There are red-stemmed *Cornus alba* varieties which grow the same way.

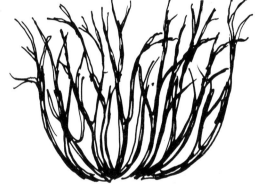

The highly decorative *Euphorbia wulfenii* creates the same bowl silhouette to a height of 85 cm (34 in) and spreading widely.

At a much lower level, the grey-leaved *Salix helvetica* grows in a bowl-shaped pattern. So too do lavenders including the cotton lavender, *Santolina chamaecyparissus*, but the necessary interference of the gardener when clipping the plants produces a rounded form.

Some of the prostrate dwarf pines can grow in a concave curve. *Pinus mugo pumilio* from the European Alps is a prostrate shrub but the branching habit is erect and branches curve upwards. Slightly bigger and with much larger and silvery blue needles, the North American *Pinus strobus* 'Nana' is strikingly like an inverted umbrella form. The dwarf pines are much used in Japanese gardens, which provide a setting in which they can look their best. The courtyard garden also suits these beautiful conifers well.

In areas where soil is acidic, a dwarf shrub, *Daboecia cantabrica*, resembling heathers, but less hardy, progressively roots outwards forming small bowl-shaped patterns. The slim upright flower stems should be cut to retain neatness. It looks good as an associate of the sun-loving rounded form of dwarf azaleas.

WEEPERS

Weeping forms are always popular. The huge *Salix chrysocoma* (weeping willow) is not suitable for the average garden but *Betula pendula* 'Youngii', (Young's weeping birch) can be a most stylish alternative as a wide-spreading weeping specimen tree. Two other silver birches, *Betula pendula* 'Dalecarlica' and *Betula pendula* 'Tristis', are narrower in profile but have trailing branches. Smaller trees like the Kilmarnock willow, *Salix caprea* 'Pendula', and *Pyrus salicifolia* 'Pendula' also have weeping forms. But both are densely round and can be clumsy mop-headed trees unless sensitively pruned to encourage arching and outward growth, resulting in a lighter grace.

Also small, reaching at most 5.5 m (18 ft) is a very pretty tree noted for its stiff weeping habit and drooping pinnate foliage: *Sophora japonica* 'Pendula' is very densely leaved but attractive when grown as a specimen, possibly in a town garden.

A very striking mulberry tree could be grown as a small but wide specimen. *Morus alba* 'Pendula' is not tall but is wide spreading. Branches support dense foliage curtains which trail to the ground.

Also unusual in weeping form is a spectacular, large, purple-leaved beech named *Fagus sylvatica* 'Purpurea Pendula'. It is a dense, sculptural 'show stopper', visually dominating and must be recognized as such.

Far lighter than any of these, *Cotoneaster* 'Hybridus Pendulus' can be grafted on to a stem and grown as a very small and charming tree. *Buddleia alternifolia* from China, can be trained as a one-stemmed small tree which has arching branches weeping prettily with pale green lanceolate foliage. In summer it is decorated with tiny lavender flowers.

Some large conifers should be mentioned. The wonderful blue cedar, *Cedrus atlantica* 'Glauca Pendula' has sweeping wide arms with long trails, which in later life need some support. Also requiring the space of a very large garden, *Chamaecyparis nookatensis* 'Pendula' has upturned arms supporting floating trails of leaves. *Picea breweriana* (Brewer's weeping spruce) has similarly balletic arms, carying trailing branchlets from upcurved branches. Less hardy, and smaller, the Kashmir cypress, *Cupressus cashmiriana* is just as theatrical. One more conifer, different because it is deciduous, but very beautiful indeed, is *Larix decidua* 'Pendula', but this tree is also only for open spaces, as its ultimate height is over 15 m (50 ft).

One or two of the dwarf conifers have very pretty weeping forms. *Cedrus deodara* 'Golden Horizon' is a pretty, fair-haired dwarf cedar. *Tsuga canadensis*

The widely weeping form of a youthful Betula pendula *'Youngii' contrasting with the erect growth of ferns and* Pinus mugo. *Below, ivy provides a lush carpet.*

'Pendula', a weeping form of Eastern hemlock from North America, is also noteworthy. Both of these grow well over large rockery boulders or in capacious planting troughs.

TOPIARY

Small leaved plants may be well formed naturally but they can also have shape imposed upon them. Topiary has been in and out of fashion for hundreds of years. The most commonly clipped plants are yew and box. The fashion is re-emerging and people are once again treating densely small leaved shrubs as a sculptural medium and having fun.

The photograph on p. 37 shows a Japanese-inspired very distinctive form of topiary where the rounded mounds seem to resemble massive water-worn boulders and create a feeling of large powerful landscape.

3
PRIMA DONNAS

THERE are some people who command an audience. With the best will in the world they cannot get lost in a crowd. Some quality makes them a star. They may be bigger and better, more beautiful, noisier, self-assured, elegant; descriptions which can be applied to the plants we choose for our plots. Even 'noisy' applies. I leave the canes and dry foliage on my *Miscanthus sacchariflorus* just because it is so communicative in winter. Think also of the aspen whispering away through the summer.

As with humanity, these exceptional plants require careful handling. The prima donnas, all strongly structured, hold the stage and the chorus is there to display, enfold and serve the giant status of the star. These eye-catching architectural plants can make the most humdrum garden stylish, provided there are not too many different examples within one visual space.

LARGE LEAVES

In the large country garden, where there is room for luxury, a jungle of *Petasites giganteus* rising from boggy soil, with their 1.2 m (4 ft) diameter leaves, is extravagantly lush. This is such an invasive plant that it must have unlimited space or be avoided at all costs.

The great *Gunnera manicata* is another even more massive waterside plant with ragged, bristling leaves as much as 1.5 m (5 ft) across. These huge rucked and puckered umbrellas belong beside lakes in larger estates rather than in the smaller private garden.

All these giant-leaved plants look magnificent when massed. They can contrast beautifully with the delicate tracery of quantities of ferns, the slim tall lines of the flag iris and at a higher level, the trailing floating leaves of the huge *Salix chrysocoma* (weeping willow), as can be seen in the photograph on p. 42. These are only for substantial gardens where a spacious waterside creates the perfect backcloth.

Much smaller and far more manageable, *Peltiphyllum peltatum*, mentioned in Chapter 1, can provide a similar effect but for more intimate spaces. Here again, damp soil is essential.

(Opposite) The unique foliage of Gunnera manicata *showing off its huge puckered leaves enfolded by soft trails of weeping willow. Reedy* Iris pseudacorus *and moisture-loving wild meadowsweet offset this massive and dominating plant.*

The large rounded leaves of petasites surround a sculpture by David Thompson.

The large cabbage-like leaves of *Crambe cordifolia* put it in the same notable class as the petasites but it will grow in dry areas and is not appallingly invasive. The heart-shaped puckered leaves create a lush, dark green mound 1.5 m (5 ft) tall, reliably hardy and providing a firm foundation for billowing clouds of gypsophila-like flowers, which are delicately hazy above the stolid foliage.

Equally powerful and with leathery leaves is an outstanding foliage plant, *Rheum palmatum* 'Atrosanguineum'. Known as ornamental rhubarb and originating in China, this rheum reaches about 1 m (3 ft) in height but spreads a good 2 m (6 ft) in diameter. The imposing deeply cut, huge leaves emerge red in spring and retain this redness on the undersides of the glossy foliage throughout the season. Feathery red flowers reach a dominating 2 m (6 ft) in early summer and create very unusual seed heads. The dramatic foliage of the rheums, splendidly extravagant in front of shrubs, creates shadows and jagged leaf patterns visible from a long way off. It is quite remarkable. The rheum requires moisture, as do so many of the large-leaved herbaceous plants.

Crambe cordifolia, *heavy with flower, displaying its rich green cabbage-like foliage.*

Lysichitum americanum (bog arum) grows in very boggy areas. Its brilliant yellow spathes appear early in the year along the muddy sides of trickling water. They look plastic amongst the more subtle green foliage of the associating bog plants. However, the later leaves are tall, over 1 m (3 ft) long, paddle shaped and green. Their simplicity of form makes the plant easier to relate to as the growing season progresses, providing a smooth cool green contrast to some of the large, damp-loving ferns like *Osmunda regalis*, or the chopped leaves of *Rodgersia podophylla* and the coppered *Rodgersia aesculifolia*.

I am rather wary of recommending that most dominant of architectural plants, *Heracleum mantegazzianum* (giant cow parsley). Unforgettable, it is actually rather antisocial. It seeds prolifically and, unless there really is unlimited space for wild gardening, can become a real problem. Nevertheless the photograph on p. 102 shows it superbly suited to its site. Here it has room to grow and is visible from a distance. There is one problem which should be recorded: the sap has been known to cause nasty skin complaints. So do many other plants, such as the euphorbias, but the blisters from the heracleum can be very painful. On the whole I think this plant is better handled with gloves.

Most of the above plants suit a more rural garden style with relatively unlimited space, often with either natural moving water or a small lake, rather than a large pool. For the smaller suburban gardens or town courtyards the prima donna plants should not be those which are uncontrollably invasive. Their architectural form will stand out more vividly in confined spaces and the surrounding 'chorus' of other planting must be the perfect foil.

EXOTICS

The military yucca, standing to attention, swords at the ready, is just such a plant. Too many of them, and the garden acquires a quasi-Riviera quality, with all the phoniness of tourist souvenir paintings, but just one yucca, or say a group of three, displayed as the main focus for a garden, can add drama throughout the seasons, heightened in summer by the magnificent plume of creamy white bell flowers. There is a very striking form of *Yucca filamentosa* named 'Bright Edge' where golden outlines emphasize the form. Another variety, *gloriosa*, is taller as it grows from a woody trunk. This is a stiff upright shrub, formal and dominating.

A similar exotic, which could have been devised on the drawing board, is the Chusan palm, *Trachycarpus fortunei*. This highly structured shrub has fan-shaped spiked leaves growing from a dark fibrous trunk. They can be as much as 1.2 m (4 ft) across. The radiating knife points catch the light and draw the eye. As with the yuccas, the allusion to more exotic subtropical floras of the world cannot be avoided. The associated plants could reflect this. Yuccas, *Musa basjoo*, or a powerful bamboo would dramatically compete for attention, but *Piptanthus laburnifolius* or *Crinodendron hookerianum* or a huge glossy magnolia would also prove to be very interesting backing. However the yucca is not a plant to hide behind others with only occasional appearances. It must be wholly visible and sited only for display. If you are uncertain, don't use it.

If, on the other hand, you are still drawn to the charms of the Chusan palm and are prepared to move a container plant inside for winter, there is an ideal compromise. *Chamaerops humilis* is a dwarf fan palm which grows to 1.5 m (5 ft) and has fanned leaves, every bit as exotic as *Trachycarpus fortunei*. It too is evergreen and has the same glossy green spiked-fan leaves. As long as it is placed in full light, perhaps on a terrace, and is grown in fertile well-drained soil, this movable feast could grace the garden every summer.

One of the most exotic specimen plants must be *Musa basjoo*, a species of banana. This plant really has to be protected well against winter extremes, even to the extent of wrapping the leaves. If this is done, the plant provides a spectacular tropical effect for large spaces. The evergreen, arching, smooth, blue-green and palm-like leaves are 1 m (3 ft) long. The whole shrub can reach 1.8 m (5½ ft) in temperate areas but as much as 5 m (16 ft) when really well suited. Other exotics can be grown companionably to create a glamorous effect — but only where space is not at a premium.

Much more familiar, but also a touch exotic, *Fatsia japonica* is a useful

The exotic foliage of Musa basjoo, *if wrapped in winter, can be grown in mild areas.*

Highly architectural, glossy-leaved Fatsia japonica *can be softened by associating with either the feathery leaves of dicentra or the simple foliage of brunnera.*

Linked dramatically, these exotic foliage shapes create an exciting planting scheme seen growing in mid-summer heat. The fanned spikes of the Chusan palm are echoed by the sword-like foliage of a red-leaved phormium and both are softened by the gently mounding underplanted geraniums and a background of the tall falls of the great Miscanthus sacchariflorus. *A blue foliaged eucalyptus is just visible behind.*

evergreen shrub which has thick, polished, deeply lobed, palmate leaves. It can grow over 3 m (8 ft) tall and spreads widely, commanding attention. It is a plant of surprises in that it would appear to be neither evergreen nor hardy. In fact the large bright green shiny leaves grow successfully in shaded areas and, though needing some winter protection and careful siting, it is certainly no weakling. *F. japonica* is used time and again in 'architecturally designed' town gardens as the large glossy leaves always add structural distinction to some rather bare corners. There is a very attractive variegated form which is worth looking for.

The handsome foliage of Ficus carica *in a sheltered site, is anchored by soft mounds of* Salvia officinalis *and ground-covering ivy.*

SMALL TREES

Not all strongly formed foliage plants are exotic in style. There are some tall shrubs which have the organized characteristics of small trees. Though they take up a lot of space, they too can add flair to a town garden, as well as making great impact in larger spaces. The Chinese *Magnolia delavayi* has huge, polished, dark green leaves with glaucous undersides. Sited against the wall of a house, or a very high brick boundary wall, it is magnificent all year round. It is important that it is grown in rich soil and that good protection is provided, as it is not one of the hardiest magnolias. The flowers are not huge but are delicately pretty and scented. *M. grandiflora* 'Exmouth' is a sturdier plant and flowers beautifully and reliably, early in its life. It too has glossy leathery foliage but with rust coloured undersides. But the leaves are not as magnificent as the 30 cm (1 ft) long leaves of *M. delavayi*.

A very fine tree which can be tailored to suit a wall or be tamed to grow in a relatively small town garden is *Ficus carica* (common fig) which has very distinctive structured large foliage. Deeply lobed and palmate, the leaves are highly decorative. Though deciduous, the fig is surprisingly hardy and, if cut back by severe weather, will even grow again from ground level. To gather fruit as well, the gardener must choose the most suitable variety for the area and observe the horticultural practice specific to the fig. This is a most attractive plant when grown in association with architecturally defined spaces, or even in containers, and although it is deciduous, I personally prefer it to *Fatsia japonica*.

Sometimes a canopy is wanted to create patterns of flickering light in a bare space, or to screen towering neighbouring buildings. There may be insufficient room for large trees but *Aralia elata* (Japanese angelica tree) takes some time to grow to 4.6 m (15 ft) and has huge bipinnate leaves growing as ruffs at the tips of the branches. Despite their 1 m (3 ft) length, they are delicate, soft compound leaves, which float in the air creating pretty lace patterns against the light. In early autumn a further crowning of lush panicles of creamy white foaming flowers trail down below the leaves emphasizing the decorative riches of the plant. The suckering growth pattern of this shrub creates a sculptural mini-forest of brown thorny stems rising from the ground. At ground level these parallel verticals are so unusual that it would be a pity to hide them behind dense mounds of foliage. Instead, low-level ground cover would emphasize the height as well as views through the stems. Alternatively, the aralia can add a lightness amongst dense shrubbery or can filter strong light from plants which must not be scorched. To see one at its best, as a specimen in a lawn creating floating horizontal patterns of giant leaves, is a joy. The two variegated versions of this tree-like shrub are extremely pretty, though slow growing and expensive.

Varieties of *Rhus* (sumachs) also provide a canopy of pinnate leaves. These are wide spreading but suckering small trees which have brilliant autumn colour, particularly *Rhus glabra*.

A densely packed very small tree from Japan *Eriobotrya japonica* (loquat), is a rich dark evergreen. The leathery corrugated but shiny leaves allow no light through but they are large and the tree can be grown as a lush 'lollipop' shape.

Amongst other small 'trees' which provide structural form in a garden, the 'tree paeonies' should be mentioned. They are really shrubby perennials but look rather like very small, many-stemmed trees. Here again, rather wayward brown stems sucker from ground level but also carry the most attractive deeply cut foliage. *Paeonia lutea ludlowii* has bright fresh green leaves and reaches a height of 1.8 m (6 ft). The bonus of huge golden yellow single flowers in late spring adds to its desirability. *P. delavayi* hybrids offer other colours. Protection from the east is important to avoid too rapid a thawing of night frost on a sunny morning. They will, however, grow in semi-shade and good rich soil to produce their lush foliage throughout the season. Placed near some of the rather sombre evergreen shrubs such as rhododendrons, hollies or viburnums they can lighten a corner. They blend with other shrubs rather well and are less dominating than some of the other prima donnas.

FERNS

Still talking of 'mini-trees' *Dicksonia antarctica* (tree fern), actually from Australia, is a wonderful fern whose fronds create patterns of mathematical perfection. This is a primitive tree whose predecessors were companions of the dinosaurs. It is certainly not a plant for every garden as it must have a mild climate and an acid, humus-rich soil.

There are other significant ferns which grow more easily. Whereas the smaller reliable ferns, such as *Dryopteris filix-mas*, and the shield ferns, blend so prettily with mixed planting in shade and in sun, some other ferns come into the prima donna category. These require space to display themselves. *Osmunda regalis*, the royal fern, is aptly named. Born to rule, it unfurls elegantly to a noble height of 1.2 m (4 ft). With its roots in wet, fibrous, lime-free loam, but the crown above water level, it associates very well with the tall flag iris and, due to its beautifully constructed foliage, compares visually even with competition from petasites. The fronds are lacy rather than frothy and glow a warm copper colour in autumn. On an alternative scale, and creating quite different proportions, the royal fern rises majestically above the smooth domesticated hostas and even makes *Rodgersia pinnata* subservient.

Equally hardy, and very elegant, *Matteuccia struthiopteris* (ostrich plume fern) also needs permanently moist soil. It grows from a narrow stem and reaches out symmetrically from this pivot, very much like a shuttlecock. The fresh green fronds uncurl with style and grace. This is a less dominant fern than the osmunda, but has finer detail. If a few are grown together, the neat, repeated fan shapes are charming, particularly when sunlight filters into the form, silhouetting and lighting the fronds. It too associates beautifully with other waterside plants but must always have room to develop.

SPIKES AND PRICKLES

Paradoxically, the contrasting stiffly prickly form of the statuesque shrub *Mahonia lomariifolia* does have a lacy, fern-like image when viewed from a

Growing in mild damp conditions, the tree fern Dicksonia antarctica *is magnificent.* Arum italicum *'Pictum' has unusual marbled arrow-head leaves.*

Onopordum acanthium *magnificently silhouetted against* Cotinus coggygria *'Royal Purple'. The soft dark red foliage and 'smoke' flowers provide a coloured and textural foil for this boldly spiked silver biennial.*

Outstandingly architectural, Mahonia lomariifolia *looks superb in shade with* Helleborus foetidus *and* Iris foetidissima.

Exotic plant association is here shown when tall Arundo donax *provide a background for spiked* Yucca filamentosa *and grouped* Hosta lancifolia.

The recurving, deeply incised foliage of the silvery cardoon, Cynara cardunculus, *displaying its stiffly vertical flower heads. This fine specimen plant dominates surrounding mixed perennials.*

distance. Reminiscent of the ferns, in the richly decorative detailed leaf patterns, it is actually hostile to touch. This is an erect evergreen shrub which grows to 2.5 m (8 ft) tall and the pinnate leaves, though prickly, create a rather rococo texture along the stately stems. The similar *M. media* 'Charity' and 'Winter Sun' are hardier and have the same worthy qualities of being suited to shade, growing on any soil and being evergreen. All of them carry terminal racemes of warm yellow flowers as a gift in winter. But *M. lomariifolia* has class. This is truly a proud individual. It is less hardy, however, so careful siting or the protection of a town garden is important. Grow it to be seen, as its architectural form is an asset all year round.

Another extremely dominating, prickly-foliaged plant is *Onopordum acanthium* (Scotch thistle). This is a biennial so must be planned for. This plant raches 2 m (6 ft) and branches widely. The photograph on p. 54 shows the broad grey leaves, silvery in the sun, backed by the rich purple-red foliage of *Cotinus coggygria* 'Royal Purple'. It is extremely spiny so not suitable for a home with young children. But for its short existence it dominates the view and is always a talking point, particularly in a lacklustre herbaceous bed.

Softer, but still spiny, the majestic *Acanthus spinosus* has long, shining, dark green leaves which are deeply divided and have spiny points. The mound of foliage is created by layers of arching, incised leaves from which the erect spiny foxglove-like flowers reach a height of over 1.2 m (4 ft). The architectural structure of the leaves has long been recognized, as they are the source of the decorated capitals of the Corinthian columns of classical Greece. Less dominating than the Scotch thistle, it nevertheless must have space for the lapping foliage to show at its best. It does, however, accommodate well to the fussier leaves of some herbaceous plants and can provide a useful contrast to the filigree artemisias or the plainer, rounded begonias.

The well known cardoon, *Cynara cardunculus*, grows in a similarly layered pattern of arching, deeply cut foliage. However, although these leaves are cleanly pointed, they are not at all prickly. This softer foliaged plant is a real star. The leaves are a gentle, silvery grey-green, elegantly curved and 1.2 m (4 ft) long. From the centre rise the branching artichoke-like inflorescences. The

The sculptural forms of Agave americana *'Variegata' well shown in company with a palm, dracaena and cactus. As this exotic sun-loving garden is in London these plants will be moved indoors for winter.*

The downward flow of the weeping birch is countered by the upthrust of the red Phormium tenax.

Acanthus spinosus *rises majestically from groups of smooth-leaved hostas.*

photograph on p. 57 shows it in splendid isolation amongst rather formless foliage. A rich moist soil is important and staking is necessary, but this imposing plant is worth growing. This is a true prima donna in that its volume and height make all surrounding vegetation subservient. It is, however, surprisingly conciliatory when displayed against the rich burgundy leaves of *Corylopsis willmottiae* 'Spring Purple' or fronted by the massed red leaves of *Sedum maximum* 'Atropurpureum'. It will enhance a group of feathery leaved species roses like *Rosa rubrifolia*, contrast with massed, pointed *Sisyrinchium striatum*, or cool down a confusion of mixed foliage patterns.

Whilst still thinking of plants which look sharp or are indeed painfully spiky, *Eryngium decaisneana*, a South American plant, also known as *Eryngium pandanifolium*, reaches an arresting 2.4 m (8 ft). The foliage presents a deceptively graceful line, though, in fact, the long narrow leaves are very sharply toothed and one needs gloves to handle it. The flowering stem, also very sharp, branches widely, carrying hundreds of elegant tiny flowers in autumn. Though it is an evergreen, this plant does succumb to frosts. However, it usually survives to live again. Much smaller and far less of a prima donna, other eryngiums are attractive plants with graphically jagged outlines. Amongst these the *E. bourgatii*, *E. variifolium* and *E. alpinum* all create richly patterned foliage, and are noteworthy specimens (see photograph p. 86).

The horizontally layered hosta anchors vertical feathery ferns and phormium as well as linking the climbing Humulus lupulus *'Aureus' to the ground.*

For sculptural effect the American aloe, *Agave americana* is hard to beat. The photograph on p. 58 shows it growing in hot dry sun. The foliage grows in a rosette formation with stabbing, pointed leaves and a rather moulded, immovable, plastic quality. In colder climates it is best grown in a large container so that it can be brought in for winter. It is not a gentle plant, and unless isolated, it can only blend successfully with succulents, like cactus and yuccas or palms and phormiums, none of which are shy or retiring.

In contrast and more human, both the cordylines and the phormiums make dramatic soloists. Both grow stylishly well in containers or make eye-catching specimens in paved courtyards or bordering terraces. *Phormium tenax* reaches 3 m (10 ft) in its native New Zealand. The smooth, grey, sword-like foliage, topped with tall, dark red, flower stems, makes this a plant for a prominent position, particularly when backed with the textured surfaces of shrubs. In cooler climates this phormium is smaller but nevertheless highly architectural in its fan-shaped symmetrical outline. The magnificent variegated and royally red varieties create possibilities for different siting. Some of the smaller plants like *P. cookianum* 'Cream Delight' or 'Tricolor' can provide very attractive visual impact in mixed borders. Alternatively, they can be most satisfactory as accent plants, when placed with formal symmetry beside steps.

HOSTAS

The hostas do have to be mentioned again. Few other herbaceous plants are quite so precise in line or sculpturally neat in layered foliage. Bergenia is untidy in comparison. The hostas can create compact regular shapes as the leaves overlap one another. *Hosta* 'Frances Williams', 1 m (3 ft) high, has large rounded glaucous leaves with biscuit-coloured margins. *H. sieboldiana* 'Elegans' also has very big leaves which are waxy, ribbed, blue-grey and heart shaped. *H.* 'Royal Standard' is also large but a bright rich green. Then there are smaller ones, such as the white edged *H.* 'Thomas Hogg' or the pointed, narrow-leaved *H. lancifolia*. One unusual variety *H. undulata*, creates a rippled pattern. Grown en masse, a group of hostas can provide dramatic groundcover. Grown as individual specimens in intimate spaces, they soften a hard landscape and bring a note of formality to a garden.

BAMBOOS

Varieties of bamboo have already been described. Many of them provide tall grassy backgrounds; perfect foil for the contrasting shapes of the rodgersia family or the huge rheum and petasites. They spread greedily, out of control, creating thickets which can be extremely difficult to remove. However, there are some which are individuals of character. *Chusquea culeou*, a beautiful 5 m (15 ft) tall bamboo from South America, grows in dense clumps and has a slender branching system. As the stems are not hollow, they can be cut and will retain their leaves in water. *Arundinaria murielae* is well behaved and can be used in medium-sized gardens. It has shortish leaves and is prettier than many of the longer leaved bamboos. There is an extremely hardy bamboo, growing to 4 m

(12 ft) which looks superb as an isolated specimen plant of stature, named *Phyllostachys bambusoides*. The broad, glossy leaves are pointed and adorn yellow stiff canes. *Sasa palmata* is a most tempting bamboo as it has huge, flowing leaves, but it is a rampant transgressor. *S. veitchii* also has graphic pretty leaves but they are smaller. The more modest, beautifully golden-striped *Arundinaria viridistrata* is a little more manageable. It can reach 2 m (6 ft) or less and the fresh leaves each season are extremely pretty. As it is invasive, it too should be kept separate from other plants, though I must confess to an accidental but alluring combination with one of my mahogany coloured day lilies.

GRASSES

Another family of specimen plants, much loved in suburban gardens, but needing to be burned back to contain their growth, are the cortaderias, the pampas grass of South America. *Cortaderia selloana* varieties are the most popular. These make immense clumps of reflexed grass-like foliage, luxuriantly surrounding the erect plumed stems. These plants must be grown in splendid isolation. Do note the ultimate size before you select.

Arundo donax (giant reed) is rather more to my liking. It is less exotic so blends well in my temperate garden. It reaches a stately 2.4 m (8 ft) and carries broad drooping greyish leaves on alternate sides. It is a statuesque plant, softened by the falls of the leaves. Similar, and already mentioned, *Miscanthus sacchariflorus* from Asia, reaches 2.7 m (9 ft) in a season and the leaves arch down in waves from strong vertical stems.

Other grasses can make good specimens. *Miscanthus sinensis* 'Zebrinus' (tiger grass) has unusual yellow bands across the blades. *Carex pendula*, the great drooping sedge, provides ornamental arching leaves and grows to a height of 1.2 m (4 ft) in shade, where it can be a valuable contrast to other woodland plants. *Stipa gigantea* is a semi-evergreen grass, 1.8 m (6 ft) tall, and adorned with oat-like inflorescences above the narrow graceful fountains of foliage. *Deschampsia caespitosa* (tufted hair grass) is another elegant grass which also has narrowly arching foliage and carries dainty plumes in summer. All these grasses need space around them. The surrounding foliage should be low, but the background could be evergreen shrubs whose flower interest is over by late spring.

SILVER-GREYS

A specimen plant with a difference, *Euphorbia wulfenii*, is unlike those previously mentioned. Originating in the western Mediterranean this is an evergreen spurge. The foliage is glaucous and grows in a rhythmical regular pattern up the strong erect stems. These are topped with citrus yellow flowers in late spring. Stems should be cut back to base when dead, making room for new ones to maintain the compact bowl-shaped growth of the plant. Growing

Opposite: Blue leaved self sown poppies, a rounded feathery santolina and a tangle of tall slim grasses are dominated by the texture of Stipa gigantea *in flower.*

Slightly tender, but elegant tall and grey leaved, Melianthus major *is an outstandingly beautiful foliage plant.*

in full sun, this euphorbia is extremely architectural in form. The plants in the vicinity should not compete but lie low or contrast with simple, soft foliage shapes. It makes a very handsome specimen when isolated on a patio thus displaying its strong architectural form.

Also needing full sun and not suited to anywhere where sharp frost or freezing wind can destroy it, is one of the most beautifully foliaged shrubs, *Melianthus major*. This sumptuous shrub comes from South Africa and has soft blue-green foliage. The pinnate leaves are serrated at the margins, about 30 cm (1 ft) long and grow with a languid elegance. Reaching 2.4 m (8 ft) in full sun, the architectural value of this lovely plant is emphasized as the light revels on the silvery sculptured form. Grown in association with blue flowers or soft purple sage, or fronting the wine red stiff berberis, melianthus provides silvery luminous romantic quality.

Macleaya cordata is another large grey-leafed plant. This is a Chinese perennial which reaches over 1.5 m (5 ft). It should not be sited at the back of the border as the beautiful grey-green, deeply lobed leaves, whose undersides are cool white, dress the plant from ground level to its full height. The flower heads are white and appear in summer. The plant associates well with both warm and cool colours and the clarity of the leaf pattern can be soothing amongst a multiplicity of textures and greens. The similar, but taller, *M. microcarpa*, the plume poppy, has fluffy pale rust-coloured flowers but it is inclined to multiply rapidly by underground colonizing roots.

CLIMBERS

Amongst climbing plants, *Vitis coignetiae* has huge leaves often 30 cm (22 in) across. It demands attention rather than providing mere background and in autumn becomes a spectacular brilliant crimson. *Actinidia chinensis* (Chinese gooseberry) also has large foliage, but without the autumn brilliance, and the hop, *Humulus lupulus* 'Aureus' also offers a challenge as its large, coarsely toothed, five-lobed leaves are a bright eye-catching yellow.

The planting around the prima donnas should be non-competitive and retiring. There is a need for sensitively related foliage patterns which will act as a subordinate background. Should other of these striking prima-donna plants be seen within the same view there must be a linking theme, for example some exotic shapes like palms, bamboos, grasses and fatsia will all look well together. On the whole these plants are better treated as specimens where attention focuses upon them. Other plants can provide a backcloth like yew, Portuguese laurel, viburnums and so forth, or act as relatively anonymous fillers such as spiraea, ribes or day lilies.

At the foot of many of these spectacular soloists a ground pattern of soft alchemilla, dicentra, brunnera, geranium or artemisia leaves can celebrate their giant status. This is particularly so in the more intimate smaller space gardens where the contrast of the strong with the gentle provides pleasurable viewing.

4
PLANT
ASSOCIATION

FEW buildings stand in isolation. Architects have to consider surrounding buildings when designing and this presents them with constraints. In a similar way the notion of creating compatible planting groups, so that individuals look well with their associates, needs thought. Such ideas are increasingly popular in garden planning. Horticultural demands make for natural companionability, for example shaded acid beds growing rhododendrons, pieris, skimmia, gaultheria and so on, make for a pleasingly natural harmony. Similarly, hot dry requirements create happy relationships between artemisias, rock roses, brooms, tamarisk, succulents and others.

The domestic garden scene is, however, an artificial concept; a mini-landscape of aesthetic relationships which is pleasing to the senses. Purely in these terms the assemblage of shapes and forms, as already identified in the previous chapters, is the crux of the matter, how to arrange plant form and mass in balance with restful areas of simplicity, making a coherent unity within the garden.

The diagrams on pp. 68, 69 show some of the visual relationships to be considered. Bearing in mind that, at all times, background and views are very influential, it is helpful to think in terms of grouping plants with certain criteria in mind.

When considering the value of accent planting, where a group becomes a natural focus for attention, then the assemblage can be complete in itself. Grouping by number is a useful way of creating sculptural units.

Sometimes a focal point can be achieved by grouping identical shapes in a non-symmetrical association, for example a group of three tall, slim conifers, like *Juniperus communis* 'Hibernica' as seen on the large sheet of diagrams. On the other hand, by repeating or echoing forms at different points in the garden, a link can be forged where the eye picks out similar shapes and makes bridging connections. In such a case a group of lace-cap hydrangeas, in flower, emphasizes the line of distant *Cornus controversa* and the theme is echoed more

A pool amongst trees looks beautifully tranquil accompanied by appropriate foliage of ferns, rodgersia, irises, hostas and bog arum.

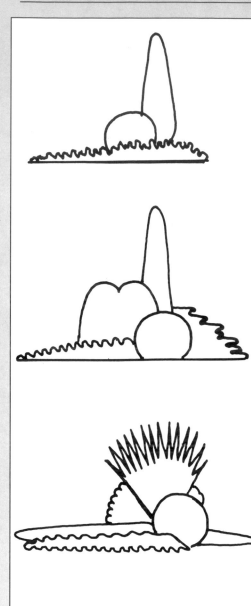

A classic combination of three forms creating a scalene triangular shape. One upright, one rounded and one lowish horizontal always makes a neat sculptural assemblage.

Five shapes together work well when there is one dominant ascendant, anchored by two rounded mounds and two horizontally structured shapes.

Five shapes again, though a smaller group, and this time the dominant form is a fan-shaped yucca or similar plant. Here again contrasting rounded forms and horizontal layers offset the dramatic focus.

Identical specimen fastigiate trees, placed in irregular but dynamic relationship. They are inescapably tied together visually but not by symmetry. Two are close and the third slightly apart.

The rhythm of a classic repeat pattern is shown here. This is a decorative group. There is no real interest in three-dimensional possibilities, unless the viewer is at one end and this is one side of an avenue.

This repeated linear pattern is totally three-dimensional in approach. The scope for enhancing perspective effects, as well as insistent symmetry leading to an undisputed focal point, can be carried out with conifers or broad-leaved trees.

A meandering, romantic informal path curves around identical specimen planting. The dynamic bridging relationship between the forms creates perfect unity with the path.

Balance created by a 'yin-yang' harmony of opposites. This is easy on the eye and neither too dominant nor self-effacing.

locally with horizontally layered conifers, like the low-level *Juniperus sabina* 'Tamariscifolia', or the taller *Juniperus media* 'Pfitzeriana' which levels and flattens in maturity to about 2.5 m (8 ft).

However, contrasts of form can add great vitality. This type of combination is also shown diagrammatically. Rounded shapes like hebes or *Cistus corbariensis* constrast with dynamic jagged shapes like *Yucca whipplei* or *Phormium tenax*. Gentler lax shapes like *Acer palmatum* 'Dissectum', or at a lower level, *Cotoneaster salicifolius* 'Gnom', can be in opposition to the vigorous uprights of *Salix hastata* 'Wehrahnii', *Cornus alba* 'Sibirica' or the fleshy-leaved uprights of *Euphorbia wulfenii*.

It is very important that the idea of contrast is not carried out to excess. No-one wants to look at a garden which is so full of contrast that the result is agitated and there is nowhere for the eye to rest. Quiet tranquil areas are as essential to the garden scene as are the empty spaces of a Japanese print.

In a completely different mode the garden plan may be more formal and symmetrical. Symmetry is not always easy to handle. It can be used as a repeat pattern, to create decorative rhythm, or used for framing and thus enhancing staged garden views, or then again provide marshalling avenues or allées drawing the eye to distant vistas. The classic Italian gardens revel in the various uses of the perpendicular Italian cypress. Usually symmetry encourages static, ordered design but, in the case of avenues, vanishing perspectives produce diagonals which inexorably concentrate the attention on one spot.

A word of caution may be useful. Where there are great contrasts of form and texture, it would be as well if there were to be a colour link. In the same way, should the contrast be that of texture and colour, some similarity of shape may be in order. In other words, though contrast might be the order of the day, some subtle bonding would prevent the scene from becoming too turbulent. A gentle link will hold the plot together.

GROUPING FORMS

This book considers choice essentially in terms of the shapes and forms created by leaves. It does not for example take into account the effects of flowers. It relates to decisions based upon orchestrating forms and leaf mass, texture and colour, aiming for a coherent unity and harmonious whole.

To create your haven there is good sense in tackling garden planning in terms of sculptural form. Some blending and contrasting of shapes can provide the rhythmical foundation of the garden. Though there are many other considerations which will influence decisions, three-dimensional forms, within fixed boundaries, will provide the framework for the planting profile. The intentions need to be clear. Later chapters make some reference to these other influences.

Number

In many gardens there are main fixed viewing points, say from a terrace or arbour, or possibly a framed view through a window or a garden arch. Sculptural groups can be created to catch the eye, as would a real sculpture. It is

The attractive lobed foliage of Hydrangea quercifolia *backs the mounded* Viburnum davidii. *Pretty spikes of* Sisyrinchium striatum *add summer charm.*

generally more satisfactory to arrange these groups in odd numbers. Even numbers suggest symmetry and formality and usually do not hold the attention but instead, lead the eye onward.

Grouping units of three

Units of three have been used since classical times as a source of satisfying composition. Shapes can be clustered to produce a most satisfactory static mass. For example, a vertical, a rounded and a spreading form always work well together. The triangular profile is restful. When one form stands alone it is eye-catching. Introduce another and the tension alters instantly but an unwanted symmetry occurs. Add a third and the group becomes a united major feature in the gardening space. A slim conifer, a rounded hebe and a spreading juniper

create an evergreen version of this grouping. Alternatively a narrow upright rosemary, a rounded potentilla and a wide spreading mass of *Stachys lanata* perform the same way but add textural and floral variety. On a smaller scale the same relationship could be achieved with *Acanthus spinosus, Pinus mugo pumilio* and a drift of thrift, *Armeria maritima* 'Alba', all growing from a cluster of pebbles or gravel.

Units of three can be very attractive when all three plants are identical. I refer again to this in the section headed 'Repetition'.

Grouping units of five

If a group of five shapes is created, repeating the horizontal line makes for stability. Weeping forms relate well to the horizontal, as weeping willows to water, but static round forms can provide a positive anchoring.

On a largish scale *Betula pendula* 'Youngii' fronted by *Cistus corbariensis* and *Hebe* 'Pewter Dome' with the mounding horizontal *Viburnum plicatum* 'Mariesii' and low level wide spreading *Prunus laurocerasus* 'Zabeliana' would provide a neat group throughout the year.

Trailing lines of racemes of Itea ilicifolia *in late summer contrast with fans of* Iris germanica *and soft rounded* Alchemilla mollis.

On a smaller scale, a group of *Paeonia lutea ludlowii*, growing approximately 1.8 m (6 ft) tall, has very attractive informal foliage. In front a tall fine specimen grass *Miscanthus sinensis* 'Silver Feather' reaching 1.8 m (6 ft) needs plenty of space around it. Complement these with some *Potentilla arbuscula* 'Abbotswood' and at the foot massed grassy foliage of *Liriope muscari*. The whole can be settled in with a ground cover surround of *Geranium lancastriense* 'Laurence Flatman'.

On a different scale again similar grouping acquires more drama if the jagged spikes of *Phormium tenax* are added amongst weeping acers, a horizontal contoneaster and groups of grey-leaved helianthemum.

Repetition

The ploy of planting groups of identical shapes can be very effective. For example using units of three identical forms, such as dense columnar conifers or classically graceful silver birches, can provide an attractive focus.

Interestingly, the units do not necessarily have to be physical companions. One could be a far distant Lombardy poplar and the other be a fastigiate beech or cherry or a tall narrow conifer. Duplicating the shape, albeit on a different scale, distracts attention from the horizontal division, creating a bridge by association. As can be seen in the diagram, the eye will make the connection. This trick can help to break immovable boundary lines. By associating shapes within and without, the dominance of the horizontal line is reduced.

Similar visual linking can be very useful when bridging across a path. Figures 2 & 3 show how a path can look natural and at ease amongst duplicated foliage patterns. A dynamic relationship across the path, linking one side to the other works well when the shapes are recognizably similar. Compare Fig. 3 where the three shapes are totally dissimilar. The result is very uneasy. There is no opportunity for the eye to find a linking bridge. Instead, the three unrelated and equally forceful shapes break the rhythm and the result is an unhappy one.

Incidentally, it is worth mentioning here that when paths are to be curved, they are always more successful when there is a reason; that is, there should be some shrub or tree which necessitates an altered direction. Paths which curve without reason look very unnatural and contrived.

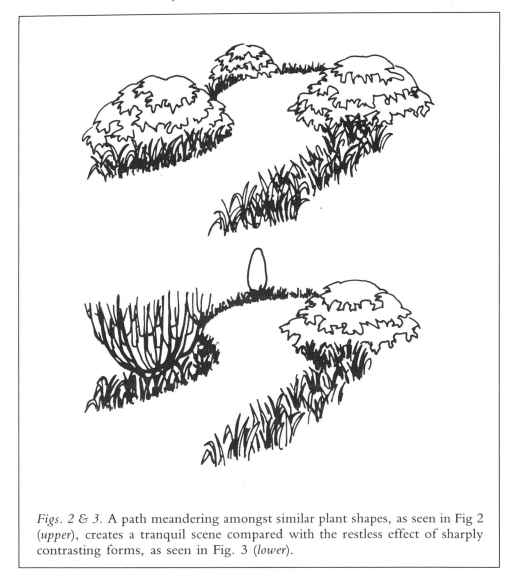

Figs. 2 & 3. A path meandering amongst similar plant shapes, as seen in Fig 2 (*upper*), creates a tranquil scene compared with the restless effect of sharply contrasting forms, as seen in Fig. 3 (*lower*).

A strategy of imitation can also be quite forceful when plants of greatly differing sizes are juxtaposed. For example consider the effect when the falls of leaves on the erect canes of *Miscanthus sacchariflorus* echo the trailing lines of a great weeping willow.

Then again, repetition of a shape can be a most effective method of distracting the eye from a problem. Figures 4 and 5 show a simple rectangular garden which was to be re-planned, but the owner wanted to keep a mature and very beautiful conifer growing absolutely centrally in the space. He also wanted an informally styled garden but thought that the tree made this an impossibility.

Figures 4 & 5 show how the eye can be deceived. By echoing the vertical forms asymmetrically elsewhere, bridging diagonals are introduced. From these, the informal sweeping curves of the lawn can be established. The eye no longer rests upon the lonesome pine but moves around the garden. The verticals are supplied by a group of narrow *Betula pendula* 'Tristis' at the far end, then closer to the onlooker, columnar conifers and erect bamboos draw attention. Emphasis on verticals can be achieved seasonally with herbaceous flowerings, such as delphiniums, lupins, cimicifuga and so on. Mellowing the verticals are rounded forms of background shrubs, like choisya and viburnum, plus horizontally tiered juniper and *Lonicera pileata*. At a lower level, foliage detail blends these strong shapes to create a garden of delightful informality.

Contrast

If there is insufficient contrast of form in the garden, the whole scene can become rather bland. By contrasting one form with another, vitality is introduced into the design. Vertical shapes can provide dramatic accents but they should be counterbalanced with contrasting horizontal or rounded forms. Structurally strong shapes are needed in all gardens but unless there is flowing, massed planting to provide contrast, the unity of the garden will be lost.

Extreme contrast of form can be very effective. One shape can enhance the other. The immense forms of the rounded gunnera are dramatic beside groves of slender erect bamboo. On a smaller scale, the accenting spikes of phormiums add great impact to the rounded mass of cistus or hebe. Similarly, but smaller again, a toothed incisive *Eryngium agavifolium* makes sharp distinction with soft mounds of *Salvia officinalis*. At a distance, in winter, a forest of erect, coloured

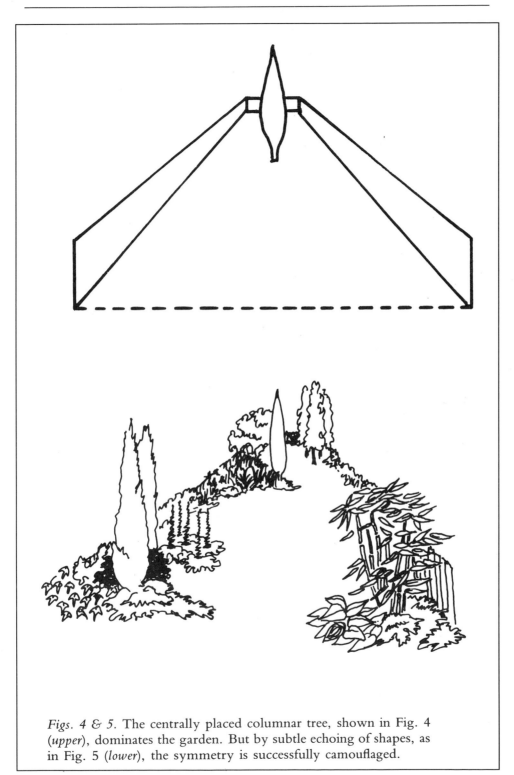

Figs. 4 & 5. The centrally placed columnar tree, shown in Fig. 4 (*upper*), dominates the garden. But by subtle echoing of shapes, as in Fig. 5 (*lower*), the symmetry is successfully camouflaged.

Cornus alba stems differ greatly from fountains of large grasses or the pendulous branches of the dwarf Kilmarnock willow covered with silvery buttons of catkins. At the base, a link can be maintained with a ground pattern of rosette-leaved *Heuchera* 'Greenfinch'.

Sometimes, massing the same shape can heighten contrast. If a number of *Iris pallida dalmatica* 'Variegata' were placed within the protection of *Viburnum davidii* this would create an almost 'Art Deco' image, simple yet stylish.

Not all contrast need be instantly visible as part of the main view. Pockets of hidden contrasts, revealed only when walking around a garden, can be charming surprises.

A simple effect where a *Cornus alba* 'Elegantissima' rises from *Juniperus media* 'Pfitzeriana' would be attractive in winter as well as summer. The bare red stems rising from the softly tiered evergreen makes a striking contrast and in summer, the addition to the cornus of very pretty, pale variegated foliage, adds extra charm.

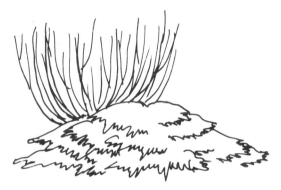

In a shaded damp area, the rising fronds of *Osmunda regalis* (ostrich feather fern) from the curvaceous lapping hostas and *Ligularia dentatum* 'Desdemona' provides another effective contrast of shapes. The hostas submit graciously to the dynamic fan-shape of the fern, enhancing its elegant uncurling fronds and anchoring it to the ground.

Groupings where one shape is repeated, albeit in different sizes, plus the contrasts of other shapes in quantity, can work very well as long as there is one powerful dominant leader. Figure 6 shows this type of composition. There are rounded forms of different heights composed of a large *Spiraea arguta*, three evergreen *Daphne laureola* and a rounded *Potentilla arbuscula* 'Abbotswood'. Nestling around these are the soft cream-yellow leaves of *Salvia officinalis* 'Icterina'. At the front, a group of dwarf lavenders are, in their turn, fronted by the rounded leaves of bergenia. At the back and dominating the group is a tall *Mahonia lomariifolia*. This prima donna holds the group together. The vertical is echoed in summer with a group of *Verbascum bombyciferum* and the erect flower heads of the lavenders. The round-leaved bergenias are in sympathy with the rounded forms of the shrubs. These plants are compatible with each other and provide an all-season flowering scheme.

It is very interesting to note how, if the dominant prima donna were to be removed (Fig. 7), the group would become far less exciting and resemble an army looking for its leader. The prima donna could of course be one of many other plants. A very tall phormium tenax, a group of aralia stems or *Miscanthus sacchariflorus* are amongst those which would be equally effective.

Often the individual beauty of form of one particular shrub is less important than its adaptability to mixed planting. The deeply cut foliage of tree paeonies frame bold ornamental grasses. Equally valuable when massed, are epimedium plants which offset the tall elegant fronds of *Matteuccia struthiopteris* as can be seen in the photograph on p. 1. Some plants, like day lilies, can blend absolutely anywhere. Their light green grassy foliage is easy on the eye.

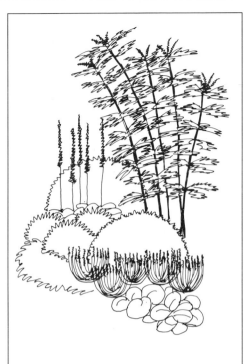

Figs 6 & 7. The planting arrangement in Fig. 6 (*above*) is striking as the Mahonia dominates the group. If this plant were to be removed, as seen in Fig. 7 (*below*), the result is acceptable but bland.

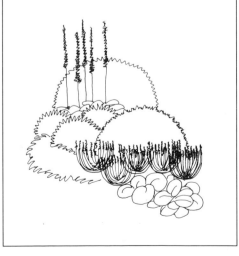

Symmetry has always had its place in a formal garden. As a path emerges from shrubbery to the open space of lawn, a pair of sentinels, such as fastigiate yews on either side, make a clear statement, as shown in Fig. 8. Alternatively, changes of level indicated by steps can be formally marked if twinned *Viburnum davidii* or dramatic yuccas are placed on either side. This sort of device has been used throughout the ages scaled to suit large and small gardens.

You may be lucky in your garden and have some old-established, random-shaped forms. Nature is rarely perfect and both trees and shrubs can develop asymmetric habits, straining for sunlight, crafted by wind or overendowed during a year of heavy fruiting. Dynamic diagonals result from such dramas. Seize on these. The most carefully planned gardens can be terribly boring unless some happy accident creates unpredictable character. In my own garden a very old apple tree has been so overladen during the years that its trunk is at 40° to the ground. It is quite beautiful, but I did not make it so.

You must also have noticed the diagonally twisted trees along a coastal route where the wind has moulded dynamic form. If one was really clever, subtle pruning could achieve such dynamism. But then we are back to the skill of the Japanese gardener.

Fig. 8. Identical shapes, visually linked across a path, mark a change of function as the garden space.

Line

In an effort to make sense from confusion, the eye continually creates alignments within the bounded space of the garden. These lines create a rhythm which can be used to direct the attention. With the effect of perspective, lines which are erect can produce a diagonal. The classic avenue has been much loved over the centuries. Attention can be drawn to a focal point, be it a vista, sculpture or gazebo. The rides of the eighteenth century used this device, luring people along a defined route to a gathering centre.

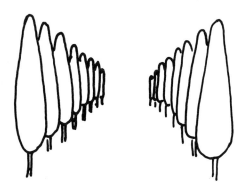

In small garden terms, perspective tricks can help to create an illusion of greater space. Placing extra large-leaved foliage near the house, making the borders converge slightly, rather than parallel to the boundaries, and duplicating shapes like fastigiate conifers at distances along the garden length progressively smaller in stature, can be useful tricks of illusion (Fig. 9). For example, echoing a tall *Chamaecyparis lawsoniana* 'Columnaris Glauca' with the very finely narrow *Juniperus virginiana* 'Skyrocket' which is on quite a different scale, and planting small trees and fine-leaved shrubs at the far end can also be effective, particularly when large-leaved ivies, hostas, fatsia or, as in the picture, *Rhododendron macabeanum* are closer to the house.

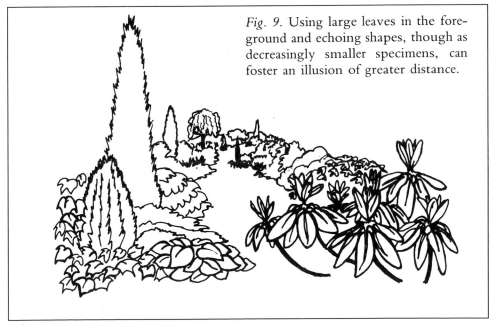

Fig. 9. Using large leaves in the foreground and echoing shapes, though as decreasingly smaller specimens, can foster an illusion of greater distance.

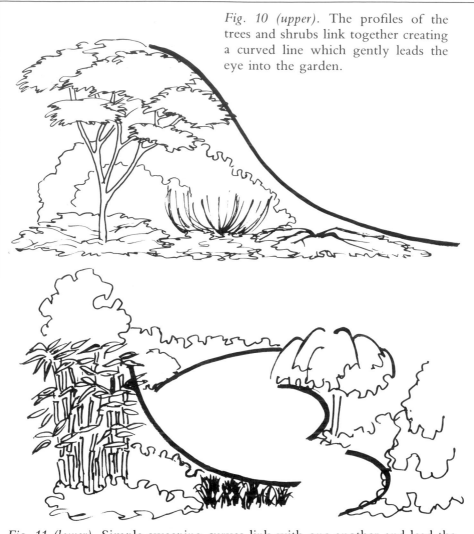

Fig. 10 (upper). The profiles of the trees and shrubs link together creating a curved line which gently leads the eye into the garden.

Fig. 11 (lower). Simple sweeping curves link with one another and lead the eye back into the garden space, except for the distant line which leads to hidden delights beyond. Linear patterns like these should not be too complex.

Less geometric, more rhythmical lines are formed by the transition from tree canopy to ground level through the layers of underplanted shrubs and herbaceous plants. This will happen in many parts of the garden. The eye follows the line down until it either rests at a focal point or picks up a relationship with other lines elsewhere (Fig. 10).

As with a good photographic composition, the eye should not be distracted out of the frame. These curves link with one another continually referring the eye back into the composition (Fig. 11).

Diagonal and curved lines create movement but in some cases a more static garden design is wanted. The vertical forms of *Cupressus sempervirens* in classical Italian gardens contribute much to the geometric harmony of this garden style.

In this diagram elegant geometry is the keynote, rather than the excitement of curves and diagonals awash with mixed planting. However, geometrical line need not be without drama. Solid rectangular masses can reveal exciting glimpses of a sunlit garden beyond.

TEXTURAL LINKING

So far I have discussed architectural form but, just as building materials have varying textural surfaces, so too it is relevant to consider these qualities with regard to foliage. Juxtaposition of one surface with another can reveal otherwise unnoticed detail. Plain smooth hostas contrast greatly with the concertina leaves of veratrum or the feathery-leaved astilbes. The fragile beauty of ferns is emphasized when placed near the round glossy foliage of *Galax urceolata* or the divided clarity of *Helleborus corsicus*.

Coarse surfaces

Amongst the larger leaves, surfaces can vary from extremely coarse to silky smooth. Some catch the light and refer it into the garden space and others absorb it, damping down excessive richness.

Two tall evergreens from the Far East, *Viburnum rhytidophyllum* and *Eriobotrya japonica* (loquat) both produce leathery corrugated foliage. This roughness provides a textural foil, flattering other more delicate surfaces. The loquat's leaves are thickly glossy whereas the viburnum tends to absorb light.

Some herbaceous foliage is particularly coarse. *Rodgersia aesculifolia* has a crinkled hessian-like bronzed surface which contrasts well with the cleanly ribbed hostas or the pretty soft leaves of dicentras. The leaves of *Crambe cordifolia* have a coarse cabbage-like appearance yet it is covered in clouds of tiny flowers in summer.

Ribbed leaves

Some leaves have engraved ribbed veins presenting a very graphic pattern. *Viburnum davidii*, always neat and dutiful, has incised lines along the elliptic leaves. So do the hostas, in some cases extremely marked, and the imposing veratrum. The frothy fronds of ferns, suitable companions for shade, are a complete contrast to this incisive veining. Alternatively, the sunny companions, *Alchemilla mollis* or silvery artemisias show to advantage against neatly inscribed viburnum foliage.

Astilbes provide a feathery contrast to the handsome foliage of acid-loving Smilacina racemosa. Asplenium scolopendrium *uncurl below*.

Richly textured bronze foliage of Rodgersia podophylla. *The strikingly jagged leaves have an ingrained leathery look.*

Shiny surfaces

Glossily smooth rhododendrons, after loosing their fabulous flowering, are a foil for pretty, unassuming ground covers such as the light green arching *Smilacena racemosa*, the running enthusiasm of *Cornus canadensis* or the shiny leaved *Maianthemum bifolium*, all North American plants.

The laurel is probably one of the most lustrous leaved of all shrubs. Its bright green polished foliage is highly reflective and creates a welcoming sight in many gloomy areas. Varieties of aucuba offer similar burnished shine. Their surface can also be richly textured with creamy-yellow dots, streaks or blotches and they will grow anywhere. The shiny leaved evergreen, *Pittosporum tenuifolium*, has the added distinction of possessing undulatingleaves which create a rippled effect. This is not a fully hardy shrub. Also not fully hardy, *Griselinia littoralis* is another evergreen whose leaves have a polished surface. Slow growing, it is nevertheless useful, as it thrives by the sea and has bright green or variegated leaves making it a pretty specimen for a town garden. I like it best with *Armeria maritima* and *Eryngium maritima* (sea holly) in its seaside home.

Prickles

Which brings me to prickly textures. Holly must be the most famous due to its seasonal connections. However, there are over 200 varieties. Permutations of variegated cream, yellow, white, pink, purple and even silver are possible. The most spiny holly of all is *Ilex aquifolium* 'Ferox', nicknamed the 'hedgehog holly', which is spiked even on its upper surface. Hollies always look attractive when associated with hellebores, Solomon's seal and ferns.

Berberis belong to another group noted for being extremely prickly. They are often used in municipal planting to restrain an undisciplined public. There are very many varieties of berberis, some of which are evergreen and prickly. *Berberis darwinii* is probably the best known. As the textural detail is densely rich the berberis benefit if grown with smooth large-leaved hostas and heart-shaped brunnera foliage in shade.

A spikily textured eryngium where the flower heads nestle within a collar of spiky sepals and the foliage is delineated with tracery of light coloured veining. The range of pale sea greens to lime greens enhance the rococco textural effect.

The New Zealand holly, *Olearia macrodonta* 'Major', is worth growing despite not being fully hardy. The prickly evergreen leaves are a soft grey with silvery white undersides and it carries pretty panicles of white daisies in early summer. It contrasts beautifully with *Cotinus coggygria* 'Royal Purple' both for colour and for the rounded smooth soft foliage.

The mahonia group is invaluable. The pinnate japonica species have been mentioned already but the Oregon grape, *Mahonia aquifolium*, must be included as this prickly and glossy-leaved shrub will grow absolutely anywhere.

From South America, *Desfontainea spinosa* is a compact shrub with holly-like foliage. It has remarkable orange tubular flowers in summer. However it will not survive extreme cold.

Stiffly growing thorny pyracantha, so often trained rigidly to a wall, can be softened at base with the grassy curves of hemerocallis or the glossy rounded leaves of bergenia. Neither are demanding and will cope with the dryish conditions of wall-side soil.

There are some prickly herbaceous plants which stand out amongst other foliage. The huge biennial *Onopordum acanthium* is a noteworthy prima donna. Eryngiums are an interesting family. They have ruffles of spiny bracts around cool grey-blue flower heads, adding a lot of character to a sunny herbaceous border. *Acanthus spinosus* with its deeply cut spiny leaves looks statuesque, growing from a sea of *Tiarella wherryi*.

Woolly leaves

For something completely different, try woolly foliage. In reality, these are leaves covered in fine silvery hairs which, en masse, appear as soft to the touch. One of the woolliest of herbaceous plants is a biennial, *Verbascum bombyciferum*. It grows to a great height of 2.4 m (8 ft) from thick woolly basal leaves and even has woolly stems. The silvery quality is enhanced against a dark yew hedge. *Phlomis fruticosa* (Jerusalem sage) also has woolly foliage but the grey is tempered with green rather than silver. Complement either plant with the texture of silvery grey feathery foliage like *Santolina chamaecyparissus* or purple-red leaved *Heuchera* 'Palace Purple'. Native to Eastern Europe, *Stachys olympica* 'Silver Carpet' is well known by its nickname 'lambs ears'. Often used to provide a pretty silver edging to a sunny border, its tactile quality proves irresistible, throughout summer, to little fingers.

The descriptive 'lanata' and 'lanuginosa' indicate woolly foliage. The small willow, *Salix lanata*, can look at home on a rockery or stylish with paving. Similarly felted, *Thymus drucei* 'Lanuginosus', provides a soft mat on hard stone or brick.

Mat-forming leaves

There are quite a few tiny-leaved plants which carpet the ground at the very lowest level. Minute thymes, chamomile, helxine, raoulia or sedums provide varying textures, some softly mossy and others more gritty. At this lowest level these varying textures are extremely attractive when used with hard surfaces.

Here the smoothly ribbed foliage of hostas and narrowly concise iris emphasize the richly detailed texture of fern fronds.

Velvet foliage

I have a liking for richly velvet textures which give a depth to colour. *Chamaecyparis obtusa* 'Nana Gracilis' is a compact conifer but it has rich depths of green due to its moss-like foliage. At ground level the mossy saxifrages create velvety mounds dotted with pink, red or white flowers in spring. Unexpectedly one of the brooms, *Genista horrida*, can clothe a rockery with dense velvet-like foliage. Mosses of course are the ultimate velvet surfaces, though disappointingly damp to lie on. The Japanese have mastered the art of using moss in the garden. It is not easy.

A contrast of opposites where vertical ferns fan out above a collar of grassy, downward flowing, falls of day lilies.

Tapestry textures

A texture which is not soft but nevertheless is richly decorative, can be found in the mass of small but distinctive identical leaves. *Lonicera pileata* is a wide-spreading low shrub. The tiny evergreen rounded leaves provide a richly textured surface which contrasts well when planted as a lacy underslip to the more sombre leaves of some of the large evergreens. There is also a golden, tall variety *Lonicera nitida* 'Baggesen's Gold' where the tiny yellow–lime leaves make a densely rich tapestry which can be allowed freedom of growth or clipped.

As mentioned earlier, *Cotoneaster horizontalis* adds to its compact textural richness by growing in a striking branching pattern. In autumn, the tiny 'button' leaves are spots of gold enhanced with dots of red berries.

Densely packed small-leaved foliage is of great use in the art of topiary. *Buxus sempervirens* 'Suffruticosa' can be clipped to any extravagant shape.

Lush grassy foliage

Amongst visually competitive foliage, a conciliatory effect can be achieved by areas of low lush dense grasses, creating pools of calm. A Spanish thrift, *Armeria caespitosa*, provides 5 cm (2 in) high hummocks of intense green grassy foliage. *Armeria maritima* is similar but 25 cm (10 in) tall. Both have the additional charm of producing flowers in early summer. In warm climates *Ophiopogon japonicus* (lily turf) provides a grassy effect. There is a dark nearly black variety named 'Nigrescens'. Far hardier, but similar, is *Liriope spicata*.

Some fine grasses such as *Festuca eskia*, a soft restful green, or *Zoysia tenuifolia* (Mascarene grass), suitable for mild areas only or treated as an annual, can both provide almost velvety grass havens in the lushness of summer.

Before leaving this section on texture I must mention some of the ivies. These are really worth looking into. Some have fine ripple effects, some are neatly pointed, some have heart-shaped foliage and many are coloured and speckled. The names tell all: 'Green Ripple', 'Curly Locks', 'Pointer', 'Ivalace', 'Little Diamond' and 'Green Feather' are but a few.

CO-OPERATIVE COLOUR

Though colour would seem to be marginal within the theme of architectural foliage it is in fact actively influential. Colour can be intensely powerful. Like music it has an instant effect upon mood. Just as the colour of building materials gives rise to sayings like 'warm yellow brickwork', 'cool white stucco', 'welcoming wood' — or, regrettably, 'cold concrete' — so too the colours we would choose for our gardens can convey so much.

However, the phrase 'a riot of colour' can mean just that. A riot is not a joyful or happy occasion but suggests conflict. Multicoloured schemes fighting for attention do not make for a tranquil scene. This is not to say that the brilliance of fairground vivacity is to be avoided. The very theme of vitality and fun does create a link between the primary colours. But probably in the garden this is not the atmosphere most wanted. As with other aspects of design it is selection which will make or break.

Some understanding of the emotional power of colour can be very useful when exercising choice. Some colours are instant attention seekers. Red is universally used to warn or to inform; whether in traffic lights or the red cross, red catches the attention. This then is a powerful colour. The young Scarlet O'Hara wanting a red dress knew exactly what she was about. Red is dominating, exciting and challenging.

In contrast, blue is a much cooler colour. It stands back in the crowd and is a more subtle invitation. Everybody likes blue.

For garden purposes you will have your own favourites. The colours inside your home frame the view outside and thus dictate some colour themes. If your interiors are subtle pastels it would be as well to avoid the jarring contrast of intense primary colours being visible through the windows.

So we have to pause. What colours are already influencing the garden? Is the architecture mellow or demanding? Is the space full of warm sunlight or reflected white light? Is it dark and dense? Are the visible neighbouring plants or views amicably green? The whole 'mise en scène' needs to be considered when colour decisions are taken.

Fortunately foliage, though offering a surprisingly large colour range, tends on the whole to be more subtly toned than flowers. There are many truly bright leaves but they tend not to have the rather alarming near-fluorescent hues of some new hybrid flowers.

Greens

Essentially most garden foliage is green, but a multiplicity of hues lies in that statement. This is the harmonious base colour for all plants. The range is great, from the fresh greens of spring to the near black green of yew or Portuguese laurel. Some greens are nearly blue such as in *Hosta sieboldiana*. Other greens veer towards yellow, creating a range of lime greens such as seen in euphorbias or pure yellow as in *Lonicera nitida* 'Baggesen's Gold'.

The dark greens, like the Portuguese laurel, make a wonderful foil for other plants. Many evergreens have fairly dark foliage and can be used to further the cause of prima donnas by not competing. Some, however, are mid-green like the choisyas or laurels; others can even be a silvery sage like *Elaeagnus ebbingei*.

The mid-greens, which are the mainstay of the summer garden, are invaluable. Shape and texture of the foliage enrich the mid-greens. They work as effectively in the peaceful garden as they do in a dramatic scenario. The fresh bright green of uncurling ferns lightens dark winter greens of hellebores, hollies and rhododendrons. The foliage of paeonies, Japanese anemones, day lilies, veratrum, and many other herbaceous plants, provides the middle layer of texturally rich greens maintaining the luxuriant vegetation of the mixed border. They can be supported by the clear shiny foliage of *Choisya ternata*, lightened by the apple green of *Griselinia littoralis* or framed by the glossy leaved *Prunus laurocerasus*, all of which are usefully evergreen shrubs.

Here the colour range of foliage is shown in great variety. There are no harsh primary colours but the scene has great vitality. Dark purple heuchera to the fore emphasized by tall red acers in the middle distance. Enclosed within are a diversity of subtle greens, blues and yellows.

Cooly beautiful jade green mounds of *Sedum spectabile* or peach-skinned surfaces of *Alchemilla mollis*, provide the elegant green of Wedgwood.

The greens are cheerful and tranquil. They display great variety due to textural effects of being glossily reflective or matt and light absorbent. Wide green stretches of lawn make gardens inviting and friendly places.

Greys

Grey-leaved foliage has become very fashionable. Its value lies in calming down 'hot' colour schemes or gently linking cooler ones. Famous 'white gardens' are often, in fact, grey foliage gardens with white flowers. The word grey actually covers from silvery whites such as *Artemisia canescens* to more leaden shades such as the pebble-like leaves of *Hebe pinguifolia* 'Pagei'. Greatly affected by light and texture the quality of greyness can vary within one plant. The silvery hairs of *Convolvulus cneorum* catch the light making the leaves silvery to white and the rosette-leaves of *Salvia argentea* are thickly woolly white in the sunlight.

A practical application of these grey-silvers is, as I said, to help lower the over-heated colours of high summer. However, rather than dotting individual shrubs in a border, it is far more effective to mass them together. Amongst reds, oranges and yellows, the grey woolly *Stachys lanata* provides front-of-border, massed edging and *Elaeagnus commutata* or *Artemisia lactiflora* provide middle-size planting for infilling.

In the case of a cooler gentler scheme of blues, creams and whites the grey leaves of artemisias help to bring out the more luminous qualities of these colours. But it is with the dark reds and pinks that grey leaves are so often used

The luminosity of the filigreed silver-white foliage of Artemisia canescens *attracts attention at the foot of a sculptured box, amongst a range of greens.*

successfully. The grey weeping pear tree looks well with the claret red *Cotinus coggygria* 'Royal Purple'. Feathery *Santolina chamaecyparissus* can be grown as a pretty silver-grey clipped low hedge around red and pink roses, although the yellow flower heads should not be allowed to develop. A very charming species rose, *Rosa rubrifolia*, is grown for its foliage which is grey with a purple tinge. An extremely rampant rose, *Rosa fedtschenkoana* has greener-grey, very pretty, ferny foliage but it is a great thorny hazard with territorial ambitions. The softer purple-grey sage, *Salvia officinalis* 'Purpurascens' can provide a very gentle low mound which also harmonizes amongst reds and pinks.

Grey leaves do not usually do well in shade but I have found that *Santolina chamaecyparissus* will cope in semi-shade conditions. Apart from practical considerations, grey-silver foliage is very important as a creator of mood.

If the garden is sunny and a romantic scene is to be set, this is where the silvery grey foliage comes into its own. The foliage colour of *Achillea argentea*, *Nepeta mussinii*, *Artemisia* 'Powys Castle' and *Stachys lanata* is grey and silver, suited for mitigating the thorns of shrub roses. The more solid forms of rounded *Lavandula angustifolia* 'Hidcote', *Santolina chamaecyparissus* and the pale pewter *Hebe pinguifolia* 'Pagei' can add structure where the romance has deteriorated to overlowing chaos.

Amongst the taller silver greys are some evergreens. *Senecio laxifolius* has leaves with white undersides which feel like kid gloves. *Olearia macrodonta* is less inviting but decorative as its grey leaves are as prickly as holly. Growing to 2.4 m (8 ft) *Romneya coulteri* (Californian poppy) has especially lush grey divided foliage. It must be grown in full sun and looks its best against a simple non-distracting background. *Melianthus major* carries its wonderful delineated grey foliage at the same height, distinguishing itself in the herbaceous beds. At a taller level the weeping tree *Pyrus salicifolia* 'Pendula' has fluttery slim silver grey leaves, above head height and so attractive when viewed from a distance.

Before leaving the greys I ought to mention an extremely pretty wide spreading conifer called *Juniperus virginiana* 'Grey Owl'. The feathery foliage is a delectable contrast amongst heavier, densely packed foliage shrubs.

Many conifers have blue-grey foliage which is often acknowledged in their names. However, size, habit and suitability are the first priorities when choosing conifers.

Blues

Blue foliage is neither grey nor green but closely allied to both. As with silver-haired grey foliage the surface of blue leaves is illusory. Usually it is a wax coating on the leaf, concealing the green and creating a glaucous smooth surface. *Hosta sieboldiana* 'Elegans' is a wonderful soft blue. Contrastingly, prickly *Echinops ritro*, the globe thistle is a steely blue. A different texture is available with *Festuca glauca*, a tufted blue fine grass. As referred to earlier, one of the bluest of leaves is *Ruta graveolens* 'Jackman's Blue'. This is so intensely blue that I find it quite difficult to place and prefer the softer grey or purple sages, as these muted shades stand out less and merge quietly. They can create a classic formal look to the garden, particularly when massed, providing an area of reticent cool tones. However they do have their place in the more romantic style of garden. *Pinus strobus* 'Nana', a dwarf pine, has very fine blue needles radiating from the stem, making this a soft romantic plant which contrasts so well with red maples.

The value of blue changes during the day as the light alters. Most of the foliage blues are green rather than red based and so merge well with green foliage. Blues are thus indecisive and subtle and can, in some lights, present an almost spectral quality.

Reds

Red foliage is very often blue-tinged except in fiery autumn. *Cotinus coggygria* 'Royal Purple', *Berberis thunbergii atropurpurea* and many of the Japanese maples provide wine-red foliage shrubs for the garden. Sometimes, as with the cotinus, the colour has an almost purple-black density which seems to absorb light, but if the shrub is grown so that sunlight filters through, its appeal becomes much warmer and gentler. Many acers carry lustrous ranges of reds, from purple to warm scarlet; often the colour varies within the same plant adding decorative value.

Dark reds can be an invaluable foil, setting off lime yellows and fresh greens to great advantage. *Corylus maxima* 'Purpurea' (purple-leaf filbert) has large rounded almost heart-shaped leaves which are a dense purple red. Being a large shrub it looks well behind delicate leaf patterns and shapes. The photograph on p. 54 shows the pale grey, spiked branches of *Onopordum acanthium* (Scotch thistle) superbly displayed against a background of claret-red cotinus.

Some herbaceous plants, like the ground running *Ajuga reptans* 'Burgundy Glow' and *Heuchera* 'Palace Purple', have an almost metallic burnished surface which can add distinction to the romantic soft-leaved geraniums and aquilegias. On the other hand, the statuesque swords of *Phormium tenax* 'Purpureum', is a highly dominant focus of attention.

The overhead dark red foliage of the trees *Prunus pissardii* 'Nigra' and *Acer platanoides* 'Crimson King' can add panache in the garden context. The dark red canopy intensifies the greens elsewhere. But restraint is better than excess, as too many dark red trees can be depressing. As I said earlier, red is a powerful colour and dramatically exciting when used sparingly, but I have seen red-purple borders looking distressingly shabby.

Some reds turn to bronze or copper as the season progresses and then, what a change of character. Suddenly even the austere garden becomes loaded with warm, vibrant yellow-reds and the plot becomes very inviting.

Yellows

Yellow is the colour of friendship. Van Gogh painted the warmth which he craved with his compulsive use of yellows. From yellow ochre to acid sulphur the yellow tints suggest sunlight, but interestingly, yellow foliage plants usually need some shade protection, as the real sun scorches the leaves to a disappointing brown. On the other hand, lack of light turns yellow into lime green, so, yet again, care in siting will repay.

This subtly coloured foliage arrangement shows the glaucous Crambe maritima *at the foot of the glowing copper bark of* Prunus serrula. *The third colour enlivening the scene is provided by golden marjoram and the lime green flower heads of* Euphorbia wulfenii.

However, there are many grasses, made brilliant with yellow colouring, which cope very well in full sun. *Hakonechloa macra* 'Aureola' has short arching leaves and is approximately 30 cm (1 ft) high. Twice as tall, and also preferring moist soil and sunshine, Bowles' golden grass, *Carex stricta*, is golden yellow. A most attractive pampas grass, *Cortaderia selloana* 'Golden Band', is extremely pretty, having falls of slim curved leaves, delineated with edgings of gold. A more softly-coloured, cream-variegated grass, *Glyceria maxima* 'Variegata', prefers rather wetter situations. This very beautiful grass grows to 1.2 m (4 ft) but colonizes greedily underground.

The hot orange-based yellows are less usual in foliage than in flowers. *Spiraea bumalda* 'Goldflame' is one exception as it begins its season quite orange-tipped and warm yellow. In contrast, the golden *Philadelphus coronarius* 'Aureus' is a far cooler yellow in spring and the two shrubs should not be seen together. However, two famously golden shrubs should be mentioned here. *Acer japonicum* 'Aureum' and *Sambucus racemosa* 'Plumosa Aureum'. Both are exceptionally lovely. Less pretty but suitable for semi-shade is *Ribes sanguineum* 'Brocklebankii'.

Lower down, the young spring foliage of *Hosta fortunei* 'Albopicta' is a glorious butter yellow edged with soft green which will brighten semi-shaded sites. As the year progresses the two colours gradually merge together. In a similar position and as edging, trailing or climbing, *Hedera helix* 'Buttercup' is hard to beat. This sunshine ivy is one of the prettiest, particularly as some of the leaves revert to speckled green. The well-known *Hedera helix* 'Goldheart' is, however, more reliable and vigorous. This wonderful evergreen climber will grow in full shade or sun and retain the butter yellow central splashes.

Of the many yellow variegated plants, I must mention *Cornus alba* 'Spaethii' with its pink-edged leaves, a lovely striped small bamboo, *Arundinaria viridistrata*, and the many varieties of golden variegated hollies as particular favourites. Golden grasses, golden maples, rich yellow elders and berberis offer different textures and shapes. The yellows are welcoming and sunny and bring an atmosphere of gaiety to the garden. Some tones can also be coolly sophisticated, for example when the hue is a pale acid yellow as in *Iris pallida dalmatica* 'Aureovariegata' or unusually marked as the *Miscanthus sinensis* 'Zebrinus'.

On a practical note, yellow gives light, which makes it useful for brightening dark corners. *Elaeagnus pungens* 'Maculata' is a tough evergreen shrub which can grow to 3.6 m (12 ft). The leaves have a central gold splash making it attractive all year round. Similarly bright, and suitable for shaded places, are some strikingly marked hollies. *Ilex altaclarensis* 'Golden King' has broad golden-edged leaves and, despite its name, is a female, so it also has berries in winter. There are many other variegated hollies which are worth looking for. Their names like 'Golden Milkboy' and 'Golden Queen' are the indicators. Some carry yellow fruit, and the birds leave these alone, unless it is a harsh winter. There are also other shrubs with yellow fruit which are worth mentioning. The crabapple, *Malus* 'Golden Hornet', and *Pyracantha rogersiana* 'Flava' are outstanding examples.

Whites

Although white is rarely seen in foliage, when it does occur it can be devastatingly effective. Another iris *Iris pallida dalmatica* 'Variegata', has creamy white-edged dove-grey leaves and is extremely elegant. The white variegated dogwood, *Cornus alba* 'Elegantissima' has frivolously light foliage cheering up the most dauntingly dark evergreens. Graciously titled, *Euonymus fortunei* 'Silver Queen', is a pale white variegated evergreen which will grow without benefit of direct sun, as will the invaluable evergreen *Iris foetidissima* 'Variegata'. White variegated leaves create a light romantic mood, even at times a slightly ephemeral quality, which can be charming. On p. 92 *Artemisia canescens* can appear silver white rather than the battleship grey of some of its peers.

There is a very pleasing low-level, ground cover plant, *Lamium maculatum* 'Beacon Silver', which grows in full shade. It too will bring light into shady corners at the foot of other shade-loving plants. The leaves are small, well-shaped and silvery white. Not strictly foliage, but worth mentioning, are the white stems of some plants. These can fit in dramatically with any foliage system. *Rubus cockburnianus* has arching stems, with ferny leaves which have white undersides. The stems are covered with a very white bloom. They arch to a height of nearly 1.5 m (5 ft). *Salix daphnoides* (violet willow) is a small tree which also has stems overlaid with a white bloom. Both plants are particularly charming in winter. So too is one of the birches, *Betula jaquemontii*, of erect, rather stiff growth habit but with a detergent-white trunk. The silver birches are of course well known. They are more elegantly shaped and consequently blend more subtly into the background.

Whites stand out in all lighting conditions and inevitably attract attention. If a punctuation is needed in a mixed border or an accent plant amongst green foliage in a town garden then white can be invaluable.

Marbled

More graphically textured variegations can be very interesting. A pleasing contrast with stone paving in the urban garden can be achieved with the marbled effect of *Arum italicum* 'Pictum', and the mottled pale green and white surface of *Hedera helix* 'Luzzii'. The prettily marked *Saxifraga stolonifera* hugs the ground at the base of trees, covering the soil and *Eryngium bourgatii* stands proudly streaked in full sun. Protected against a wall, evergreen *Pittosporum* 'Irene Patterson' is delicately marbled and tinged in winter.

It is useful to note that not only can colour manipulate mood but it can also deceive the eye. As reds advance, blues recede. In both large and small gardens such attributes can be useful. Reds, oranges and strong yellows flaunt themselves across a space of lawn, where the shy blues and mauves retreat. The effect of light ought also to be considered. Within a smaller space, as evening shadows gather, blues become intensified whereas the darker reds become far more reticent. Thus the spatial use of coloured foliage can have very practical applications.

One further word about colour in the garden. On the whole, sweeps of colour are far more effective than small patches. Greens are usually massed, but a few insignificant spots of greys, yellows or even reds will be weak. The occasional solid punctuation of dramatic colour can be extremely effective as long as the multicoloured dotted effect has been avoided.

5
STYLE

MANY gardens are planted lovingly but without any clear intention except to please. Sometimes the gardener is vaguely disappointed with the result but not quite sure why. If you have a definite aim in mind then choosing and placing plants becomes easier and often more rewarding.

If, at the outset, gardeners think about style, this may help to clarify the purchasing and planting process. The homes we live in are mostly the result of an architect's or builder's plan. They may be severely modern, crisply classical, cosily cottagey or welcoming but functional.

The garden too can have a character of its own. Is it to be a quiet and restful haven or romantic and mysterious? Perhaps a highly formal display is wanted, or possibly dramatic theatricality, or a comforting 'wild' nostalgic garden. Style is important in creating unity.

Nevertheless, whatever the character of the garden, scale and proportion must be considered. Large areas need big shapes to balance generous spaces. Leaf masses should be significant, shapes should be bold and distinctive and contrasts need to be decisive yet simple. Note how the huge-leaved gunneras look so well across an expanse of water.

The scale of trees and shrubs should also be sensibly relative to the area of the garden. However, if the garden is small, the scale needs to be cut down to suit. In town, the area may of necessity exclude the outside world and be inward looking. Appropriately sized plants will need to be more contained in their growth and their decorative detail interesting at close quarters.

FORMALITY

In the past, both geometric formal discipline and fluid casual 'natural' gardening styles have been adopted with equally decisive conviction. At times Nature has been firmly kept out, or made available only through vistas framed and selected by the garden planners. At other times, however, gardens have been seen as 'natural' landscapes, full of irregularities and apparently random views. Fashion continually changes so that, in some cases, gardens of different styles have actually been overlaid one upon another, just as new fashionable façades and extensions can conceal the original structure of old houses.

The classical setting of columns and balustrade is served well by the old gnarled twisting wistaria.

Formality in the garden has been around for a long time. The ancient gardens of Persia were devised on strictly formal rectangular patterns. So too were the cloister gardens of the monasteries, the parterres of France and the enclosed gardens of Elizabethan England, all of which obeyed geometrical principles of order.

Formal gardens tend to have straight paths, views of significant focal points such as statues, seats, urns etc., and a clearly structured, often symmetrical, layout. Sometimes the formality can be austere. At Knightshayes Court in Devon, U.K. there is a yew-enclosed rectangular garden which is furnished with stone bench seats, a statue, a large circular still pool, carpeting green grass and a specimen weeping silver pear tree. This minimalist design is tranquilly beautiful.

On the other hand, straight hedges and paths can be used to contain exuberantly textured foliage. The fashionable herb garden is nearly always treated formally. Few herbs grow tidily and many are rampantly invasive, but the textural variety of the tall hazy fennels, *Foeniculum vulgare*, compared with the thick felted leafs of mullein, *Verbascum thapsus*, or the arrow-headed upright leaves of sorrel, *Rumex acetosa*, look better when retained behind the traditional rigidly defined boundary hedging of *Buxus sempervirens*. Some herbs can themselves be treated in a formal manner as clipped hedging. These include *Santolina chamaecyparissus, Lavandula spica* and *Rosmarinus officinalis*. Chives, *Allium schoenoprasum* or clove pinks, *Dianthus caryophyllus*, can also make attractive and neat edgings between paths and herbs.

The ultimate formal herb has to be the sweet bay, *Laurus nobilis*, which can be clipped into the most wonderful pyramids and lollipops. It can be grown as symmetrically placed sculptural forms or as a single specimen. Traditionally they are often paired in containers on either side of entrances.

In larger spaces where the garden may be compartmentalized, the strictness of yew or compliant topiary can give structure to an arrangement of rectangular herbaceous or rose beds with grass paths, arches, with possibly a geometric pool or sculptural focus. Repeated shapes at symmetrical intervals can reinforce the formality. An avenue of pleached limes, a stilt hedge of hornbeam, identical small mop-headed acacia trees in corner sites, or, in milder areas, the clipped *Quercus ilex* (holm oak) from the Mediterranean, can all reinforce the formal ground pattern as vertical accents.

In a similar manner, arches along straight paths, directing the onlooker to a framed focal point, also reinforce the geometry. They can support climbers or be of living material. Laburnum trees can be pruned and arched to create a magnificent living tunnel.

Amongst foliage plants which lend themselves to formality has to be the yew. As already described, this conifer can be cut with near-mathematical precision. Other clippable shrubs like box, privet, pyracantha and holly can also achieve rectangular form, but the larger the foliage, the less geometric the outline.

Some plants which grow in naturally neat sculptural shapes are in demand for a formal garden style. Hebes, *Viburnum davidii*, conifers and phormiums all have strongly formed silhouettes. The spiky-leaved *Mahonia* 'Charity', is stylishly formal, and so too is the dramatic yucca and the large-leaved fatsia. The smaller clipped shapes of lavenders and *Santolina chamaecyparissus* all help to reinforce geometric tidiness. Some of the acid-loving shrubs like the smaller rhododendrons, skimmias and pieris provide naturally neat habits and spreading junipers and dwarf conifers look well in formal town gardens. Amongst herbaceous plants, irises, kniphofia, lilies, crocosmia, spiky veronicas and salvias grow with distinctive clarity of shape. The neatness of hostas, the rosettes of heuchera and the tidy mossy saxifrage mounds make trim edgings. Backcloth patterns of regular leaves like those of the Cherry laurel, the Portuguese laurel, choisyas and elaeagnus, provide neat evergreen boundaries.

However, even in the most formal gardens some relaxed shape such as an asymmetric *Acer japonicum* or some lush floppy foliage patterns should be considered to avoid a rather sterile result.

Courtyard gardening is often planned on formal principles to relate to the architectural lines and blocks around them. The paved layout has to be practical, as much is required in terms of leisure as well as beauty. The planting needs to be in sympathy, though the inclusion of some unexpected flamboyant exotics, like the Chusan palm (trachycarpus) a fig tree or an out-of-scale magnolia, can add great distinction. Chapter 5 develops this further.

ROMANCE

The romantic garden with its overtones of honeysuckle, roses and lavender will always have appeal. In today's rather manipulated world and with the increasing importance of 'greening' there has been a return to the idea of 'wild gardening'. Flower-power ideals have created a wistful notion of cottage gardens, wild flower meadows and even the charm of unkempt gardening disorder. In truth all these garden styles require knowledgeable management to retain any appeal. Given this, the 'random' appearance of romantic gardens can produce the most beautiful and alluring vistas.

On the whole it is easier to maintain some formality immediately next to the house to carry the geometrical links through. But progressing away from the paved functional areas, perhaps through arches, one can happen upon the curves and bountiful planting of the romantic scene. The view should be incomplete, with hints of hidden groves and screened vistas. Without being sentimentally rustic or revealing Xanadu pavilions, there can be much scope for the enticing garden of mystery. Concealment is a major part of romantic garden style. Viewing gaps reveal glimpsed spaces beyond. Alternatively, arches allow inviting light into the immediate vicinity.

The other features of this type of garden style usually include pergolas, random-shaped pools, curving paths, summer houses and statuary in arbours. The accompanying foliage must have structural content to provide a skeletal discipline. Evergreen shrubs and tall trees will link the land with the sky. Some flowing lines formed by weeping and trailing shapes, on both a large and a small scale, seductively lead the eye where they will. Soft-leaved plants move in the breeze. Relate these to flat areas of dappled lawn or shimmering water and

This gloriously romantic scene is overflowing with foliage riches. The grass path follows alongside a water course and vanishes amidst giant heracleum, petasites, golden elder and grey-leaved willow.

you are on to a winner. If the land also undulates or you have some wind-twisted trees you are indeed fortunate.

The planting for romantic gardens can be bold and gentle at the same time. A skeletal discipline of evergreen shrubs and tree shapes, so clearly evident in winter, emphasizes the lushness or fragility of other foliage. Magnificent magnolias, free-growing tall slim conifers, the dark depths of yew or elegantly arching *Cotoneaster salicifolius floccosus* are widely differing mid-height evergreens which can serve in this capacity to very good effect.

Of the deciduous trees requiring space to grow, the birches are of distinct romantic value. Consider a group of *Betula pendula* 'Tristis' swaying in the wind, a solitary specimen of *Betula pendula* 'Youngii', which weeps from widely stretching branches, or the white-stemmed *Betula jacquemontii*, palely gleaming in winter. The Judas tree, *Cercis siliquastrum*, forms a rounded crown and has huge heart-shaped leaves. However they appear late and drop early. *Cercidiphyllum japonicum* (Katsura tree) also has a rounded form but carries the prettiest small heart-shaped leaves which progress from pink to cool sea green to yellows and pinks in autumn. The well-known dark red copper beech should be planted for future generations as should the oaks, many of which have more variation in leaf shape and colour than is usually supposed.

At a lower level *Cornus controversa* 'Variegata', is a very pretty shrub, with horizontal tiers, but space is needed to allow the branches to extend gracefully.

The tall majestic *Melianthus major* graces the romantic garden scene with large pinnate and serrated grey-green foliage. It is a perfect foil to denser, more solidly packed shrubs. Planted to blend with soft blues, pinks and whites or contrasted with deep reds, this graceful prima donna is fetchingly romantic. It also looks well amidst lush green foliage surroundings, but some soft greys, like *Salvia turkestanica*, pale achilleas or silvery artemisias should be included to reflect the grey tones. Silvery leaves always further the romantic cause in the garden. The varied textures of feathery *Anthemis cupaniana*, the incised lush foliage of *Cynara cardunculus* or the sword-like grey-green *Iris germanica* leaves enliven foliage patterns.

Variegated foliage also adds lightness and charm to the romantic scene. Among herbaceous plants, variegations can be creamy as well as white. The large creamy-green leaves of variegated comfrey, *Symphytum uplandicum*, glow in semi-shaded situations and suit the character of the wild garden. *Actinidia kolomikta* provides a pretty tapestry of white, green and pink leaves on a wall. Being evergreen, variegated and silvered, pittosporums are useful as well as pretty, but they need a sheltered site. The variegated *Cornus alba* 'Elegantissima' beside the white florets and incised foliage of *Hydrangea quercifolia* is almost bridal in association.

Both grey and variegated foliage should be placed with care. Too much and the romantic effect becomes merely messy.

A most appealing quality of plants which are grown for their foliage is that of movement. Leaves which rustle or sway, like the slender grasses, or gently lift in the wind, like the velvety leaves of *Hydrangea villosa*, create an air of uncertainty. The fluttery yellow leaves of *Robinia pseudoacacia* 'Frisia' and the rippling waves along a beech hedge enhance the romantic appeal.

Though the herb garden is nearly always formally constructed, herbs can also be associated very successfully with other foliage plants in a more casual manner. The grey, purple or yellow-leaved sages make soft rounded edgings for borders. The architectural *Angelica archangelica*, a very large biennial herb, has thick ridged columnar stems, supporting the ribbed vaulting of the flower umbels and has deeply dissected green leaves. It contrasts effectively with the hazy green and red fennels, or stands tall amongst the herbaceous melange.

As supplements to wild gardens the hairy-leaved borage, structured caper spurge and vertical foxgloves can be allowed to seed. However the wilder, romantic gardens can quickly become dissolute. To hold the 'carefree' planting scheme together and link the curves and random spaces, judicious planting of informal or clipped hedges can be very useful. *Rosa rugosa* makes a romantic, dense, albeit sometimes dishevelled, hedge. Not only are the roses and hips colourful but the rather coarse foliage turns a glowing gold in autumn. Semi-formal hedges like beech and hornbeam can be clipped to maintain clarity of form and their rippling broad leaves make them softer than privet, holly or yew. On the other hand, the rectangular clipped yew adds great glamour to any garden. The dark depth provides a wonderful foil and there is great potential for creating architectural shapes with windows, arches and even small-roofed lodges.

MODERN THEMES

Contemporary garden designers are exploring all manner of new ideas. Nowadays gardens are often designed on a 'theme' principle. By choosing an idea or theme the gardener has restricted himself and, as I have discussed, any means of assisting us to select and reject, are extremely helpful in the creative process.

In terms of planting, foliage has reached a high point in importance. All-foliage gardens are not uncommon. The richness of variety has been demonstrated in this book and designers are not slow to take advantage. The photograph on p. 10 shows how effective this theme can be. Plants like hostas, which have clear form and pattern, are in great demand. Others, like *Alchemilla mollis* can increasingly be seen everywhere, used as easy, but charming foliage fillers.

On a tall scale the value of plants for their foliage form and structure has increased in proportion with the decreasing interest in summer bedding plants. Large structured plants like *Onopordum acanthium* and *Crambe cordifolia* have become highly fashionable. Other, smaller leaved but equally lovely plants like geraniums, euphorbias, hellebores, sages and ferns are grown as much for foliage as for flower. The hebes have also become a major part of contemporary foliage gardens. Another increasingly popular style, using dwarf and spreading conifers, reflects the modern necessity for easy-care gardening.

An interest in 'wild gardens' has created enthusiasm for re-evaluating what a previous generation would have called 'weeds'. Foxgloves, comfrey, even wild invasive chicory have been welcomed in. Large leaves like petasites, peltiphyllum and flag irises are now massed as important parts of a garden plan. The diversity of rodgersias and use of ground-covering euphorbias is appreciated as they integrate so well into the wild theme. Even *Heracleum mantegazzianum* can be seen in suburban gardens, but knotweed is now outlawed. I am sure that this theme of wild gardening is still at the kindling stage. The green movement encroaches upon gardeners, and there is more to come. People are choosing to grow nettles to encourage wild life. What would the gardeners of the 1920s and 1930s have said! We have certainly not yet reached the apex of this fashion.

In the United States there is a famous garden area which is devoted almost entirely to grasses. The decorative potential of these, though long recognized in mixed planting, is now being developed, so that the varieties of grasses, from the huge bamboos to the small *Briza media* (quaking grass), become an end in themselves. Enormous diversity within one group is thus explored fully as a source of style.

Similar exclusive restrictions, like limited-colour gardens, are now almost commonplace. Famous 'white gardens', consisting of much grey-silver foliage, are being imitated. There are gardens which are in a yellow–blue range and others restricted to reds, pinks, purples and greys.

Another contemporary image is that of purposefully collected 'sets'; that is collections of every variety and species of one genus. A collection of astilbes, produces not just the pretty and familiar foam flower, but also a great variety of richly ornamental foliage patterns.

The ultimate modern garden style has now reached the nadir of contemporary visual arts. A complete banning of any living material whatsoever has been carried out as a garden style. As with nihilistic experiments in painting and sculpture, this seems to be a necessary stage to be gone through. The result is really architectural space or an experience of being inside a large sculptural form. I think that probably gardens should involve vegetative material, but in this instance there would not be a leaf in sight.

For minimalist perfection, the Japanese style of garden has been traditionally developed over centuries. It is very difficult for western culture to understand

The romantic greys and silvers of Macleaya cordata *and* Stachys lanata *frame a pretty rustically designed seat beside an old brick wall.*

the balance and harmony of such gardens. The religious philosophy is so completely at one with the designing of Japanese gardens that we can neither fully comprehend nor imitate wholly successfully. Given this, we can nevertheless admire and 'borrow' ideas. Indeed there are well known and accepted Japanese gardens outside Japan. This style of gardening mastered the architectural forms of foliage a long time ago. The glorious pines, whether huge or creeping, are used for their superb form and texture. Bamboos are deployed for their statuesque qualities and great diversity of height, colour and leaf shape. The elegance of habit and exquisite foliage of the maple family is explored to the full. Where necessary, form has been sculpted, not as in the geometric abstracts of European topiary, but to make forms suggesting landscape; hills, mountains, valleys, boulders are all implicit in the clipped shapes of box shrubs. Even the humble privet has been shown to be stylish. Imitation of nature became in practice an improvement upon nature. Trees and shrubs are twisted and moulded, creating unique shapes, to be significant and dramatic within the garden.

Here again we can adapt these images to suit our own plans. The European tradition of espaliered and cordoned fruit trees or pleached limes, is based on the same principle of making natural shapes conform to our will. Oriental images, however, seem less geometric and create random forms, as if subjected to the vicissitudes of nature — but helped a little.

It is now possible to have in your garden, plants from vastly different parts of the world. Amongst the plants referred to as 'prima donnas' are plants from China, like the Chusan palm and from Australia like the tree fern. The pampas

Steps lead down from a woodland setting to a verdant glade and pool.

grass is from Argentina, the cornus family comes from countries as far apart as Siberia, Manchuria, North America and the Himalayas. The popular hebes and phormiums come from New Zealand. Bamboos are mostly from Japan and China but *Chusquea culeou* comes from South America. Fig trees grow wild in countries from Syria to Afghanistan. From South Africa the list of garden plants, now adopted all over the world, is endless. The plant hunters and horticulturalists have produced a treasure-trove of riches for the gardener's delight.

Of course none of these plants seems exotic in its own environment. I have friends in Johannesburg who would give much to be able to grow successfully, the humble *Paeonia officinalis* 'Rubra' or thalictrum or gypsophila, none of which seems exotic in London. However, there is great fun to be had in combining exotic-looking foliage plants together under a temperate sky and they can be extremely stylish. The range is necessarily limited. Many tropical plants are particularly architectural in their foliage and growth habit, but cannot be grown out of doors unless the climate is kind. Nevertheless, combining large-leaved exotics in a smallish town garden, for example, can be dramatically effective. Yuccas, palms, fatsia, bamboos and grasses play a big part. Include the acanthus, rheum, cardoon, phormiums and in shade, hostas, ferns and hellebores, and a very striking pattern of leaf shapes emerges. Top this with a canopy of fig leaves, aralia or rhus, and the near-jungle effect of green shapes is lush and enveloping.

If there is a damp area, the opportunities for exotic foliage increase. The massive paddle-shaped leaves of the American bog arum contrast superbly with large fronds of the royal fern. Ligularias add great variety of form, having rounded leaves as well as large heart-shaped toothed ones. The gunnera and petasites families may be too large, but as an alternative, *Peltiphyllum peltatum* has round leaves which are 30 cm (1 ft) in diameter. A colonizing *Polygonum campanulatum* carries attractive leaves and pink flowerheads at a height of 1 m (3 ft), though do beware of its colleague, *Polygonum cuspidatum*, which is completely uncontrollable and very tall. Rodgersias should be included in this grouping as all their foliage shapes are distinctive amongst other plants.

In any garden some grey foliage would add distinction. *Macleaya cordata*, clothed with palmate grey leaves from ground to 2 m (7 ft) and *Melianthus major*, also carrying exquisite silver-fingered foliage to a similar height, bring contrast into the garden. Some golden foliage, particularly *Hakonechloa macra*, a Japanese grass and *Miscanthus sinensis* 'Zebrinus' from China, plus yellow hosta leaves would add brilliance. Variegation may be added but I suggest that, as there will be so much emphasis on leaf forms and texture, the effect could be ruined if it is. As always, resist gilding the lily.

The style of the garden can be set almost accidentally when the gardener follows his or her inclinations. Even so, I suggest that it is desirable, for the most satisfactory outcome, to reflect on the chosen style and the best means of consolidating it.

6
FOLIAGE WITH ARCHITECTURE

FEW gardens are entirely without any form of 'hard landscape'. Paths, steps, paved seating areas, boundary walls and fences, pergolas and gates are likely to require integration at some point. Choosing sympathetic or camouflaging foliage can maintain the balance of function and design.

HOUSES TAKE ROOT

New houses surrounded by debris and cracked subsoil are a mournful sight, but it need not take long to humanize the buildings by accompanying or clothing them with leaf textures and shapes. Older houses may already have a happy relationship with the green world around them as gnarled wistaria winds its way up the façade or perhaps a clinging virginia creeper adds its glossy even texture to the house surface.

The huge leaves of plants like *Actinidia chinensis* are not ideally suited to house walls but the neater *Hydrangea petiolaris* or toothed leaves of *Schizophragma hydrangoides* are both self-supporting and are blessed with cream flowers. The beautiful blue Californian lilacs offer many varieties of flower and leaf: the hardy *Ceanothus* 'Delight' is an evergreen wall shrub which does require some support and pruning. It prefers a sunny wall as does *Cytisus battandieri* which has the prettiest silky grey leaves and pineapple-scented yellow flowers.

At base, if no wall shrubs or climbers are wanted, a house can be anchored to the ground by the fanning form of *Cotoneaster horizontalis* or more formally clipped pillars of pyracantha. Matching forms such as the fastigiate yews can act as sentinels on either side of an entrance. At a low level, wide spreading junipers, grey leaved *Hebe pinguifolia* 'Pagei', soft foliaged geraniums, clipped *Santolina chamaecyparissus,* the silvery-leaved *Anthemis cupaniana*, lacy froth of *Dicentra formosa* and the sea green leaves of *Alchemilla mollis* make attractive softening foliage.

The opaquely pale grey of the clapboard cottage is enhanced by a softly grey-purple leaved vine, Vitis vinifera 'Purpurea'.

On the shade side of the house the small evergreen *Euonymus fortunei* varieties, delicate epimediums, ribbed hostas, glossy bergenias and silvery lamiums fulfil the same purpose. Some free-standing shrubs of erect habit could be planted beside the house, if there is space. The architectural form of *Mahonia lomariifolia* or evergreen *Garya elliptica* both provide vertical emphasis. *Athyrium filix-femina* is a gentle fern which will cope in dry shade as will *Polypodium vulgare*, which is smaller. Ground layers of *Vinca minor* 'Variegata' or small-leaved ivy varieties will add creamy colour and textural variety.

CLOTHED WALLS

Not all climbers are suitable for house walls, but boundaries can have more informal sprawling plants. The huge-leaved ivies, *Hedera colchica* 'Dentata Variegata', *Hedera colchica* 'Sulphur Heart' (Paddy's pride) and others, provide self-supporting dense cover on walls and fences. The smaller-leaved *Hedera helix* 'Goldheart' is neater and will grow in sun or full shade.

Two evergreen clematis which have totally different leaves and the bonus of flowers are both worth planting and protecting. *Clematis armandii* is a vigorous climber with glossy dark slim leaves. *Clematis cirrhosa balearica*, (fern-leaved clematis) has delicately divided leaves which are bronze tinted in winter. The pink and white flushed leaves of *Actinidia kolomikta* always cause comment and, like the huge lobed yellow leaves of the hop, *Humulus lupulus* 'Aureus', must be grown in sun for best results. These various climbers all provide rich wall tapestries which will make the severest garden secluded.

To create a more three-dimensional wall cover, include shrubs such as the dark *Garrya elliptica*, silvery *Cystisus battandieri,* shiny green *Choisya ternata*, large-leaved *Fatsia japonica*, coarse-leaved *Viburnum rhytidophyllum* and some interesting hydrangea shrubs such as *Hydrangea quercifolia*. Elaeagnus, escallonia, viburnums, hollies and many other shrubs all add textural and three-dimensional vitality along boundaries. Additional possibilities are the pittosporum family with their subtly coloured and textured varieties, the huge glossy magnolias and the large-leaved, handsome common fig, *Ficus carica*.

The architectural forms of espaliered or cordoned fruit trees can be extremely fetching, skeletally in winter, and providing tapestries of texture and colour throughout other seasons. For scents, but requiring protection, *Chimonanthus praecox* (winter sweet) has spicy scented leaves, *Myrtus communis* has dark glossy foliage and is highly scented in summer and *Lippia citriodorus* has deliciously lemon-scented pale green long leaves.

FOLIAGE AT YOUR FEET

When it comes to paths, steps and paving, foliage patterns and forms can soften and enhance the architecture. The more impressive a flight of steps, the more dramatic the associated leaves can be. Formal phormiums or clipped yews stand guard, trailing tumbling ivies or vines can flow over a balustrade. Varieties of *Acer palmatum* and *Acer japonicum* look wonderfully elegant beside or cascading

The fresh green of a specimen fern with trailing vine and ivy look well with restored brick and the old sculpture.

over steps. The low *Pinus mugo* adds oriental distinction to courtyard gardens where clipped box, paeonies and iris will continue the theme. In shade, small and large ferns look well with stone which is covered in lichen; particularly worth considering is the smooth hart's tongue fern, *Asplenium scolopendrium*, as well as its more usual feathery companions.

Small-leaved trailing ivies or *Lysimachia nummularia* can attach themselves to the risers of steps, running along under the overhanging treads. Small pockets of button-leaved spleenworts (ferns) are very fetching. As with most of the hard landscape planting, foliage cover should be controlled in order that surface materials are still visible in places and parts of the risers of steps can then be defined by shadow.

Edging alongside paths can link paved functional areas with verdant plant borders. There are so many interesting foliage plants which are effective. I can mention only a few. The grey *Stachys lanata* has velvety soft texture and grows in full sun. Totally different is the dense mid-green grass-like foliage of montbretia or the softly rounded foliage of lady's mantle, *Alchemilla mollis*, with its foaming lime green flowers. In damp shade, astilbes have firm ferny leaves and hostas have layered clean-cut leaf shapes. Dicentra leaves are graceful though will not last through summer, and heuchera grows in neat rosettes. All of these leaves soften the edges of paved walkways. *Arum italicum* 'Pictum' adds its interesting marbled texture and arrow-shaped foliage in cool semi-shaded areas contrasting with the quite different rounded, wavy-edged, bronze-coloured *Saxifraga fortunei* 'Wada's Variety'.

In expanses of paving, likely to be used for eating 'al fresco', large planted groups of mixed low junipers, acers, yakushimanum rhododendrons and skimmias with a group of *Sedum spectabile* 'Autumn Joy' can be effective all year round. Lower mounds of helianthemum, parahebe, and iberis offer different foliage textures but should be certain of sunshine.

Alternatively, carpeting plants such as thymes, acaena, frankenia, helxine and pratia increase over the years covering slabs and pavers with soft treadable foliage textures.

ENTRANCES AND EXITS

There was an architectural fashion in the 1960s for designing entrances so subtly linked with window patterns that a stranger could be embarrassed and uncertain. This ridiculous state of affairs is no longer fashionable but worth noting. Entrances and exits should be clearly marked and one way of being sure of this is by using distinctive foliage.

The large leaves of Actinidia chinensis *trail over the red tiled verandah of an old Essex farmhouse. Glaucous leaved valerian and dwarf lavender nestle at the edge of the brick paved floor.*

The most obvious method is formal, symmetrical planting. Arches and clipped hedges are instantly effective. Matched symmetrical planting suits a formal gaden well. As always the yews are ideal markers, but symmetrically sited hebes, clipped hollies, skimmias or sword-shaped plants like *Yucca filamentosa* 'Bright Edge' are also neatly formal alternatives.

For the less structured garden style asymmetrical planting with visual links can be charming but still effective route markers. In a partly shaded site *Choisya ternata*, with a festooning climber behind and a dense group of low grasses like *Carex morrowii* 'Evergold' at foot, could be visually linked across the path with the shrub, *Cornus alba* 'Spaethii', underplanted with clumps of the strap-leaved *Iris foetidissima* 'Citrina', and the evergreen ground cover of *Waldsteinia ternata*. On both sides, *Euphorbia robbiae* would cover any remaining ground with dark evergreen rosettes and lime yellow flowerheads in late spring.

A similar asymmetrical scheme in full sun could have grouped grey-leaved *Rosa rubrifolia* on one side, *Viburnum sargentii* 'Onondaga' on the other, low rosettes of heuchera lining the path on both sides, silvery *Artemisia* 'Powys Castle' around the viburnum and clumps of bright reedy *Hemerocallis* 'Whichford' footing the roses, further underplanted with dwarf, grassy dianthus.

Of course some exits do need to be hidden. The 'secret garden' has great appeal, but this is an exception. Mostly we need to know where the entrances are and enhance them.

Neat bergenia and iris leaves edge steps in a town garden.

7
WORKING WITH WHAT YOU HAVE

IN previous chapters I have indicated that choices will be constrained by circumstances. None of us work upon a completely blank canvas. By considering two extremely different garden types one can see how planting forms might be developed appropriately. The large country garden and the city back yard are at opposite ends of the spectrum but both contain elements of foliage design which will be applicable to other types of garden.

LARGE COUNTRY GARDEN

Linking shapes and patterns over an expanse of land can be difficult. The transition between the intimate scale of domestic areas and the greater spaces beyond should not be noticeable, so thoughtful choosing and siting of plant material can help to create overall harmony. Beside the house, foliage can be detailed and richly contrasting, but in the longer views, planting should be massed with fewer contrasts and some clear simple forms.

The larger area creates a need for generous shapes and masses. The tree line will provide the basic profile. Most are familiarly rounded or domed but some have distinct characterful form. Fastigiate trees are those which are slim and narrow. Many conifers conform to this shape though some do 'fatten up' with age. Those noted for their slimness throughout their lives include the wonderfully dramatic *Calocedrus decurrens* (incense cedar) and the classic Italian cypress, *Cupressus sempervirens*. On a much smaller scale *Juniperus virginiana* 'Skyrocket' is extremely narrow, so is notable only in more intimate places. Many of the easily grown hollies develop into distinctly erect shapes as does the beautiful *Eucryphia* 'Nymansay', which prefers acid soil and careful siting.

Amongst deciduous trees, the Lombardy poplar, much loved by the French, shows the classic fastigiate form but is not suitable unless your country garden really is big; this tree should not be planted anywhere near buildings. Much more in scale with the average-sized country garden are a maple, *Acer rubrum* 'Scanlon', a beech, *Fagus sylvatica* 'Dawyck' and the smaller, blossoming trees

(Opposite) A house in the country is framed by the silhouettes of pines and the trails of weeping willow. The water surface is broken by lily pads and surrounded by imposing gunnera and reedy irises.

Prunus 'Amanogawa' and *Malus* 'Van Eseltine'. The unusual foliaged tree *Gingko biloba* and *Liriodendron tulipifera* 'Fastigiatum' also have slim erect forms.

Weeping trees have already been mentioned in earlier chapters but I would add two conifers, *Picea breweriana* (Brewer's weeping spruce) and the deciduous larch, *Larix kaempferi* 'Pendula', both of which are valuable as specimen trees.

Wider than it is tall *Catalpa bignonioides* makes a fine large-leaved backdrop for a country garden. There is also a particularly wide-spreading hawthorn, *Crataegus crus-galli* (cockspur thorn) which would suit the wilder country garden. *Paulownia tomentosa*, also wider than it is tall, adds an exotic touch when its heliotrope panicles of foxglove-like flowers appear in spring. Also garlanding the garden in spring, a very fine ornamental Japanese cherry, *Prunus* 'Shimidsu Sakura', is desirable for its wide-stretching arms from which hang clusters of pure white flowers.

The unruly countryside beyond can be included in the garden plan. Tree profiles offer opportunities to duplicate the shapes, thus entrapping them within the visual pattern. Garden plants like hawthorns, the guelder rose, dog roses and elders can be mixed with more tidy shrubs to invite the countryside in.

Vistas are important in the large garden. The broad sweep of massed planting patterns incorporating some evergreens, should be enlivened with very striking individuals. The large leaves of *Rheum palmatum* 'Atrosanguineum' cannot fail to be noticed. Tall biennial *Onopordum acanthium*, luminous and a spiky pale grey, stands well above other vegetation. Swathes of the pale variegated *Cornus alba* 'Elegantissima' look well with dark red berberis foliage and carry masses of upright glowing red stems in winter. Clumps of bamboo creating forests of canes make a fine backcloth for large groups of *Aruncus sylvester* and *Rodgersia aesculifolia*.

Focal points in large spaces are an asset. They introduce a sense of order, a place for the eye to rest. The focus could be distinctive, architecturally shaped plants: the tree fern, *Dicksonia antarctica* and the palm *Trachycarpus fortunei* create an exotic feel; specimen cortaderias in an island bed of grasses are unusual. Spiky *Mahonia* 'Winter Sun' and comely tree paeonies are other possibilities.

Sculptural effects of grouped arrangements can attract attention. Clipped columnar yews, *Taxus baccata* 'Fastigiata', either dark or golden, can lay a foundation for planting groups such as those described in Chapter 4. Echo the vertical lines with tall herbaceous plants like verbascum, acanthus, delphiniums, irises or veronicas and contrast with horizontals such as wide ranging maples, lace-cap hydrangeas, lengthy *Prunus laurocerasus* 'Zabeliana', herbaceous *Sedum spectabile* and the equally flat-headed achillea flowers.

Alternatively, provide a focus by choosing just one specimen tree with notable form like the spruce and larch referred to earlier. or consider *Prunus subhirtella* 'Pendula Plena Rosea', an elegantly weeping cherry tree, or *Fraxinus excelsior* 'Pendula', the twisted mounding weeping ash, both of which have enough class to hold the attention, even in winter.

The focus may be man-made, such as an arbour or summer house, which, with the use of considered planting, will merge with their surroundings. Evergreen backing, such as the dark *Prunus lusitanica*, glossy *Escallonia macrantha*, the coarse-leaved *Viburnum rhytidophyllum*, or perhaps clumps of bamboo, offer quite different alternatives. An overhead maple, like the silver maple, *Acer saccharinum*, or the walnut tree, *Juglans regia*, can create patterns of shade. Bold foliage at a human level such as *Phormium tenax* or *Rodgersia podophylla* suit the geometry of garden buildings, making them less obtrusive.

At a middle level, as seen in the photograph on p. 102, massed petasites and heracleum dominate the surrounding vegetation. The size of these magnificent plants, so notable from a distance, can be dwarfing to the passer-by, but the redressing scale of trees and tall shrubs, like willows, restores equilibrium.

The cabbage-like leaves of *Crambe cordifolia* make a distinctive mass of dark green foliage which contrasts strikingly with the giant reed, *Arundo donax*, the vertical canes of *Miscanthus sacchariflorus* or the curved grass falls of the striped *Miscanthus sinensis* 'Zebrinus'. To maintain winter interest, but without summer plumage, the evergreen bamboo *Phyllostachys nigra*, luxuriantly leaved and with black canes, skirted with the invasive patterns of *Sasa veitchii*, makes similar elegantly linear patterns.

The rural garden should have flowing lines, harmoniously related and counter-balancing forms with lush textural pattern. Drifts of colour and contrasting massed leaf shapes should be of a size to be seen easily from a distance. Topography, light and wind can all be an asset when planting rural gardens.

CITY BACK YARDS

Modern town gardens tend to be inward looking. Privacy is all and the attention stays within the space. The scale is intimate and reassuring and sometimes extremely small. The town yard must nevertheless function as external living space as well as being a secluded visual haven. Shade and dry soil may be problems but this is balanced by the asset of protection from extreme weather conditions. The microclimate of the yard may make it possible to grow some more tender or exotic plants. Mobile contained plants add to the adventure as they can be brought in when the weather worsens.

Strong planting can make the smallest space exciting. So choose this first. Small trees such as *Sorbus vilmorinii* or *Sorbus* 'Joseph Rock' have distinctive pinnate foliage which creates dappled shade. Heavier shade is provided by the wide spreading *Rhus glabra* and *Aralia elata*, both of which create magnificent canopies. On the other hand, if more light is needed a more fragmented canopy is preferable. The Australian gum trees fulfil this requirement. They also offer unusual evergreen glaucous foliage. Probably the hardiest is *Eucalyptus gunnii* which is also fast growing. Rather slower to start but prettier, *Eucalyptus niphophila* is highly ornamental and nearly as hardy. The bark is attractively marked and the mature leaves are long and narrow.

The internal space will acquire much character if some choice prima donnas are selected. In semi-shade the lush bamboos add rustling greenery, though choose less invasive ones. Allied to strong architectural geometry, bold planting, such as a large and dominating *Fatsia japonica*, or stiffly powerful *Phormium tenax*, with underplantings of smooth hostas, textured geraniums and

Growing from strong stems, the huge compound leaves of Aralia elata *float above glossy bergenia and soft geranium foliage.*

delicate epimediums can balance the strong shapes. Reinforce the verticals at a lower level using irises, kniphophia, lilies and grasses. Add a low wide-spreading *Cotoneaster salicifolius* 'Repens' and for textural contrast, also low and wide, *Pinus mugo* specimens plus some round-leaved bergenias, thus establishing good 'bones' for the design.

Alternatively, for damper more shaded conditions, choose the bold leaves of the rodgersia family or even a massive *Rheum palmatum*, assisted by the tripartite leaves of *Helleborus corsicus*, reedy *Iris foetidissima*, and the softer foliage of astilbes, brunnera and pulmonaria varieties. Include some elegantly arching *Polygonatum giganteum*, varied textures of ferns and, at ground level, runs of ajuga, lamium and *Lysimachia punctata*. Adding primulas, lilies and Japanese anemones will bring in some colour.

However, conditions may well be dry in the protected town garden. Many of the prima donnas revel in dry sunny spots. *Euphorbia wulfenii, Trachycarpus fortunei, Acanthus spinosus, Phormium tenax, Melianthus major,* the tall grasses of miscanthus and the knife-edged yuccas are all sun worshippers. Silver and grey foliage comes into its own in sunny spots. The woolly *Stachys lanata*, silky *Convolvulus cneorum*, feathery *Anthemis cupaniana*, glaucous *Sedum spectabile*, plus the artemisias, lavenders and aquilegias will provide varied low level planting opportunities. Green choices are many: amongst these the soft jade green of adaptable *Alchemilla mollis* and geraniums; the spiky eryngiums and echinops; grassy plants like the festuca varieties and *Liriope muscari*, reedy shapes of iris and agapanthus, plus rock hard small sedum and sempervivum, all contribute textural diversity.

At this point I should mention some foliage plants which require acid soil and are suited to town gardening. *Gentiana asclepiadea* (willow gentian) arches out gracefully from the centre, making beautiful patterns at ground level or in raised beds. For cool shade the trifoliate trilliums and *Cornus canadensis* from North America have a bonus of flowering as well as having neatly shaped leaves. For rounded leaves in shade, *Galax urceolata*, also a North American plant, is evergreen and glossy. These are all woodland plants and belong in the larger spaces of country gardens, but, provided they are controlled, the foliage patterns are really valuable in the intimacy of enclosed spaces. The other acid-loving familiars, such as dark glossy camellias, yakushimanum rhododendrons, neat skimmias and glowing pieris, are all tidily suited to the urban garden.

Clipped forms can be used to emphasize rectangular formality. Pyracantha can be clipped to blanket a wall so that only windows and doors can be seen. Alternatively, neat columns and horizontal lines can be formed by the same plant to reveal the beauty of old brickwork. Escallonia can also provide clipped formality for walls.

SITE CONDITIONS

Although I have said previously, this is not a book about horticultural method, some comments are relevant regarding the physical conditions which apply to your plot as they influence the choice of foliage.

Raggedly dominating, Rheum palmatum *is a handsome plant. The softening falls of hemerocallis leaves do not compete.*

Shade gardens

Firstly, a shady garden, so often lamented, is in fact a rich source for good foliage plants. So many of the larger leaves cannot cope with full sun, unless their feet are in water.

At ground level, the great variety of ivies now available, can bring colour and brightness to dark corners, as can *Lamium maculatum* 'Beacon Silver'. Contrastingly, *Ajuga reptans* provides red-purple and metallic-looking foliage and *Vinca minor* (periwinkle), will also add light to dark areas as there are variegated forms. *Euonymus fortunei* is a small shrub. It is evergreen and will grow in shade, providing neat ground cover at the bare-legged foot of taller shrubs.

An outstanding evergreen herbaceous plant *Iris foetidissima* 'Variegata' produces few flowers but has white-green stripes, which are elegant and highly visible in full shade. The plain version has glossy mid-green leaves. It is also evergreen and provides solid clumps of rich strap-like foliage, enlivened in winter with brilliant orange seed clusters. Harmonizing with these wild irises, *Brunnera macrophylla* has large heart-shaped leaves making wonderful ground cover patterns. Hellebores are glossier and have crisply shaped foliage. In contrast, epimediums are delicate rather than bold. Asarum and galax can add rounded patterns where the soil is suitable.

The grass, *Carex pendula* (1.2 m (4 ft)), will also grow in full shade and has lush foliage with arching stems supporting drooping flower heads. At first you will be delighted, but soon a great many little carexes appear and you realize that you will never be rid of this family. However it does look well with hellebores and hostas. The latter are of course of very great value in the shade garden. The diversity of shape and colour has already been discussed.

No shade garden is complete without ferns. These add a rich brocade of texture, which is invaluable as many other shaded leaves tend to be smooth and simply shaped. Here again there is much choice and many varieties have already been covered.

At shrub level, prickly hollies and highly architectural mahonias add spiky profiles. Neat forms of prunus, like the glossy laurel and the Portuguese laurel provide background cover. In the darkest, most miserable part of the garden *Mahonia aquifolium* and *Ruscus aculeatus* will survive. So too will the invaluable aucubas, which offer some vividly red berries in winter as well as a variety of leaf shapes and colour. *Aucuba japonica* 'Salicifolia' has long narrow leaves and there are also some bright gold-variegated aucubas. Look out for the cream and yellow spotted *Aucuba japonica* 'Crotonifolia' or *Aucuba japonica* 'Picturata' which has creamy-yellow splashed centres on its leaves. *Elaeagnus pungens* 'Maculata' is another evergreen, golden-yellow variegated shrub which will grow and glow in shade.

Rhododendrons, camellias and skimmias do well in shade, provided the soil is not too dry but is acidic. If these conditions exist, *Pachysandra terminalis*, in both plain and variegated form, provides a very attractive ground cover.

Exciting plants like bamboos, rodgersias, peltiphyllum, and veratrum will add great style to shaded gardens but must have reliable dampness at root.

Fatsia japonica is also on the dramatic side. This is truly invaluable in shaded town gardens. Its offspring, × *Fatshedera lizei*, sharing its parentage with ivy, is usefully hardy. However, the palmate glossy, if leathery foliage, is smaller and less vigorous than that of fatsia. The plant is apt to flop, after a promising start, and is rather spineless compared with its parent.

Combinations of these plants, using linear foliage as a slim contrast to the broader and palmate leaves, can make the shade garden a surprisingly easy proposition. This is yet another case where restriction of choice can be of such great assistance in attaining a harmonious end.

Hot, dry gardens

This is a more difficult type of garden to create satisfactory foliage composition. Many large leaves crumble miserably if exposed to heat. The look of this sort of garden will be less lush but nevertheless stylish.

Yuccas, agave, tamarix, phormium and the cardoon leap to mind as the plants for hot dry areas. Many fleshy leaved plants can retain moisture, hence the success of the house leek, sempervivum, when exposed, apparently waterless, on roof tiles.

As I said, these plants tend to be on the dramatic side. Others include *Eryngium agavifolium*, a 1.5 m (5 ft) sharply toothed plant which has dramatic outline, as has *Echinops ritro* (globe thistle) which is nearly as tall and possesses spiny-tipped, leathery leaves, and the succulent *Euphorbia wulfenii*, always an eye-catching feature.

The strictness of these very architectural plants can be softened by the juxtaposition of *Centaurea ruthenica*, a plant growing up to 1.2 m (4 ft) which has finely cut, dark green foliage, or *Bergenia cordifolia* and *Bergenia crassifolia*, which have glossy rounded foliage, surprisingly coping well with full sun. The gentle and pretty *Alchemilla mollis* (lady's mantle) will also grow in these hot rather arid parts of the garden as will the variety of foliage textures provided by most of the geranium family.

Glorious silver and grey foliage plants positively preen in hot sun. Fine artemisias, whether tall, like *Artemisia ludoviciana*, a 1.2 m (4 ft) native of North America, or small, like the mossy silvered *Artemisia schmidtiana*, a Japanese plant of a mere 10 cm (4 in), are plants which enhance others wherever they are placed. With a totally different leaf shape but still silvery grey, *Ballota pseudodictamnus* carries arched stems to a height of 60 cm (2 ft) covered with rounded distinctly button-shaped felted silver leaves. On the other hand, *Crambe maritima*, seen in the photograph on p. 95 has wavy glaucous leaves which make superb generous low-level foliage at the base of its more strident sunny peers. Silky *Convolvulus cneorum* provides yet another different texture. Helichrysum is a genus which is familiar to those who like dried flowers. Quite different, however, is the well known curry plant, *Helichrysum angustifolium*. It is a dwarf rounded white-grey shrub, similar to the santolina. *Anthemis cupaniana* is a particular favourite of mine as it has white daisies above pretty silver filigree foliage.

Plants like these perform a major role in hot planting groups as they cool down heated flower colour but more importantly they provide drifts of silver-grey throughout the growing season, even when water is in short supply.

Amongst the shrubs which thrive in these conditions cistus play a major part. The neat *Cistus corbariensis* at 1.2 m (4 ft) tall, has small white flowers, red buds, neat dark evergreen foliage and is one of the hardiest as well as the prettiest of the genus. *Cistus crispus* has sage-green foliage, contrasting rather well with its magenta flowers, but is only 60 cm (2 ft) tall. *Cistus* 'Silver Pink', however, is 1 m (3 ft) tall and has soft greyish leaves and pale pink flowers.

Also rounded in form, and thus a contrast to the prima-donna stalwarts, are hebes. Some are very small like *Hebe* 'Quicksilver' at 15 cm (6 in), some have very fine leaves and are known as the whipcord hebes, such as *Hebe armstrongii*, reaching 60 cm (2 ft). Some hebes are quite tall and have slim longer leaves, like *Hebe salicifolia* which reaches 1.2 m (4 ft). They thus offer great textural variety as well as strong outline. Smaller shrubs like *Helianthemum* (sun roses) are useful at low level and, when massed, provide rounded low shapes of silver or green leaves with the bonus of extremely pretty long lasting flowers.

Less tidy, but a suitable neighbour in the hot dry garden to both cistus and hebes, is *Phlomis fruticosa* (Jerusalem sage). The felted whitish foliage is 1.2 m (4 ft) tall and mixes well with other shrubs, as the branches are inclined to flop, unless supported. Grasses like *Millium effusum* 'Aureum', *Festuca glauca*, the stiff *Helichotrichon sempervirens*, pennisetum and stipa varieties create contrasts or softening patterns amongst the strict hebe and cistus shapes and reedy *Sisyrinchium striatum* adds further interest. Woolly plants like *Stachys lanata* and *Nepeta mussinii* are important, as so many of the sunny plants are rigid and spiked. Mat thymes, scented rosemary, golden marjoram and hazy fennel are all decorative culinary herbs which suit the occasion and the rock hard sedums, in variety, provide edgings of grey, green and red.

The look of the hot dry garden is thus very different from the shaded damp garden. Silver-greys predominate, distinctively stiff exotic shapes are also characteristic but amongst them some softening feathery, fine-leaved and woolly foliaged plants blend in. There are many more suitable plants and it is worth experimenting.

Water gardens

So far I have not mentioned water gardening but as a source of architectural foliage, it should be included.

Pools may be formally rectangular or circular, that is, have precisely marked geometric outline. Alternatively they can be 'natural' amoebic shapes, blending into a country garden. In the latter case edges are not defined but lost among boggy areas, filled to overflowing with marginal planting.

In either case, all the foliage is emphasized by the flat plane of the water surface. If the water is still, the flatness is reinforced with smooth lily pads or the contrasting oblong, floating foliage of *Aponogeton distachyos* (water hawthorn).

From this plane, vertical strap-shaped leaves, like those of the common flag, *Iris pseudacorus* and the sweet flag, *Acorus calamus*, pierce majestically elegant

Attractive mixed foliage forms in which the blue simple hosta shapes skirt the rounded-leaved ligularia which, in turn, leads the eye to the striking variegated leaves of Iris pallida dalmatica *'Variegata'.*

from a shallow depth of about 5 cm (2 in). Both have very beautiful variegated forms. The great water dock, *Rumex hydrolapathum* also provides strongly vertical accents. Many irises, having narrow vertical leaf forms, associate superbly with water. So too, do the rushes, like the tall ornamental rush *Cyperus longus*, the zebra rush *Scirpus zebrinus*, the flowering rush *Butomus umbellatus*, and the invasive typha family; these rise elegantly from a shallow depth of water, and when reflected, almost double their length. The giant *Typha latifolia* reaches 2.4 m (8 ft), thus suiting only the larger pools where gunnera and petasites act as effective counterbalance.

Along the margins of pools many of the lush foliaged plants, referred to in other chapters, look their very best and create luxurious patterns. The tall American bog arum, *Lysichitum americanum*, and its shorter relative *Lysichitum camtschatcense* at 1 m (3 ft), both produce enormous simple leaves, unusually perpendicular to the ground. Also from N. America *Pontederia cordata* (pickerel weed) has handsome spear-shaped foliage. These strongly simple images contrast well with the narrow rushes and irises.

Horizontal layering of hostas and the round leaves of *Ligularia dentatum* 'Desdemona' also provide a good foil for the verticals. As texturally rich contrasts, damp-loving ferns like *Matteuccia struthiopteris*, *Osmunda regalis* and the smaller 60 cm (2 ft) *Athyrium filix-femina* (lady fern) plus the 45 cm (18 in) *Onoclea sensibilis* all contribute fresh green lacy or fretted foliage patterns. The ferns unfurl, crozier-like, to form eye-catching fan shapes rising amongst the horizontals of the hostas and ligularias, but less insistently linear than the irises.

Amongst other foliage forms, which look so good with water, are the stately and important veratrum family, the various shapes of rodgersias, the coarse-edged wide heart-shaped leaf of *Ligularia* 'Gregynog Gold' and texturally rich astilbe foliage. It is important to mass plants like these rather than have a mixture of everything in small 'spots'. The effect is lost, unless the planting mass 'reads' clearly across water.

The overall associate with water has to be the great *Salix babylonica* (weeping willow). However, where the pond is small, formally rectangular, or near the house, an alternative must be found. A pruned Kilmarnock willow, *Salix caprea* 'Pendula', would be suitable, but rather stiff. Instead, the elegant habit of *Acer japonicum* or *A. palmatum* varieties look very pretty when associated with water. If a taller tree is wanted, the airy elegance of a weeping silver birch, *Betula pendula* 'Youngii', would also hang over water in a most dramatic way.

This chapter has discussed some possibilities for three distinct garden types. Every garden is individual and will have its own character, assets and problems. By simplifying I have included ideas for foliage which can be drawn from, and developed, within the context of your garden. The essence of most gardens falls within the categories of town or country. Special requirements and desires will need thoughtful planning. However, the general principles of selection of foliage still apply.

8
CONCLUSION

INEVITABLY, gardens are highly personal. As with our house interiors, what pleases one does not please another. There are a few gardens which do seem to have universal appeal, such as those of Kyoto or the Villa d'Este. Similarly, there are universally respected architectural works like the Taj Mahal and the Parthenon, but on the whole, as with all the visual arts, preferences are subjective. So your own garden will have its own style and choices of plants. I have set out to show that the diversity of shape, line and texture in the world of foliage is considerable. Some of the groupings and individual plants discussed may appeal and may provide some stimulus for change. I have been unable to omit my own prejudices and am only too aware that these will have changed next year, but therein lies the fun.

Those who love plants can never resist experimenting and exchanging cuttings. These will grow and space will be needed for them. They are memories of people, of places and of times. The garden is a richer place to you personally because of them. Perhaps they don't quite suit but keep them anyway. Part of the charm of the art of the oriental carpet is the imperfection, the deliberate mistake, making each one unique, as is your garden. Feel encouraged by Picasso's statement 'Taste is the enemy of creativeness' and, if you like them, retain your experiments and gifts.

Anyway, gardens are never static. This is one art form which changes through the day, through the month, through the seasons and over the years. Buildings, if they are let alone, change little. Perhaps a mellowing of tone, or colour or a streaking of pollution affects their surfaces but the structure persists. This is not so with the structure and texture of foliage plants. The garden is in a continual state of flux and will never be completed, thank goodness!

PUBLISHER'S ACKNOWLEDGEMENTS

The publishers are grateful to Freya Billington for permission to reproduce the photographs on pp. 1, 9, 49, 95 & 98. All the remaining photographs were taken by Bob Challinor.

The line drawings on pp. 21, 22, 28, 31, 47, 48, 50, 53, 55, 56, 59, 64, 71, 73, 84, 118 and 120 were drawn by Michael Jefferson-Brown. All the remaining line drawings were drawn by Jill Billington.

INDEX

Page numbers in *italic* refer to the illustrations